HER HAND IN MARRIAGE

Biblical Courtship in the Modern World

DOUGLAS WILSON

Canon Press
MOSCOW, IDAHO

Douglas J. Wilson, *Her Hand in Marriage: Biblical Courtship in the Modern World*

© 1997 by Douglas J. Wilson.
Published by Canon Press, P.O. Box 8741, Moscow, ID 83843
800-488-2034

01 00 99 98 97   9 8 7 6 5 4 3 2

Cover design by Paige Atwood Design, Moscow, ID

Printed in the United States of America.

Unless otherwise indicated, Scripture quotations are from the New King James Version of the Bible, © 1979, 1980, 1982, 1984, 1988 by Thomas Nelson, Inc., Nashville, Tennessee.

ISBN: 1-885767-26-9

For Ben and Bekah, whom the Lord
has blessed with covenant grace . . .
vinculum matrimonii

Her Hand in Marriage

Table of Contents

Introduction

> There are three things which are too wonderful for me,
> Yes, four which I do not understand:
> The way of an eagle in the air,
> The way of a serpent on a rock,
> The way of a ship in the midst of the sea,
> And the way of a man with a virgin.
>> *Agur, son of Jakeh*
>> Proverbs 30:18–19

> We like holding hands and pitchin' woo. . . .
>> *Merle Haggard*

> Sittin' on the front porch just a swangin'. . . .
>> *Stevie Ray Vaughn*

Everyone dates. Or at least, everyone is supposed to date. Or, if they don't date, then something is wrong, or someone is ugly, right? But in America today, relationships between boys and girls, men and women, husbands and wives are a stretcher case. The fact that pride exists at the heart of this problem can be seen in our various responses to the difficulties. The worse our troubles get, the more faith we have in our methods and procedures. Like the woman in Luke's gospel, the treatment we receive from our physicians does not really touch or heal our condition. And like that woman, our livelihood is now up and gone (Luke 8:43). The starting point for most of our marriage relationships, the modern recreational dating system, can be safely considered as bankrupt.

Consider how our system works. A young man notices a girl who attracts him. He asks her out, and she agrees. They start going together, and one of two things happens. Either they like each other or they don't, and both possibilities bring problems in their train. If neither one likes the other, then they both have had a bad experience. If they both hit it off, then the eventual temptation to immorality is strong, *especially* if they happened to pair off young—fourteen, say. "Glad you kids like each other! Now don't touch anything for eight more years!" "Okay, Mom!" And of course, if one is interested in staying together and the other one isn't, the possibilities for emotional snarls and interesting complications are almost endless.

If the young man and woman see one another more than just a few times, it is very easy for them both to drift into what can be called the *zone of vulnerability*. This zone of vulnerability is that place where one cannot leave the relationship without being hurt. At some point in a relationship, the man or the woman will come to the place where, if they break up, they get hurt. Once people are inside that zone, they are vulnerable. As long as he or she is outside that zone, they are not threatened at all by the relationship—it is still only a potential relationship. And, of course, in a relationship, the *degree* of vulnerability they feel toward one another will depend upon a number of factors. If a couple only went out three or four times, there may not be much damage—that will come after they each have seen twenty people three or four times. Some things accumulate. With another couple, if they have dated for three years, have been good friends, and have not behaved themselves sexually, a break-up is nothing less than a divorce without attorney's fees.

This means, of course, that a married couple is as far inside this zone of vulnerability as they can get. There is no way a couple can divorce without devastating both of them in some way. God hates divorce; His Word naturally provides the protection against the kind of damage which proceeds from disobedience. Consequently, God does not permit us to get into this zone without building a fence of protection around us. That fence is a covenantal oath; it is what we call a *marriage*. A covenant of permanent and faithful sexual union is made before God and numerous witnesses; the man and woman each declare that they are going to go together into this zone and *stay* there. They will live there for the rest of their lives.

But in our culture, men and women are trained to harden themselves so they may go readily from relationship to relationship. Sometimes there is a marriage oath made and broken, and sometimes not. Going from one relationship to another has become a national pastime. People start very early with recreational dating, and, protests notwithstanding, most dating today leads to a sexual relationship. In this regard, the pattern of behavior among young people who are professing Christians is not much different from that of the world. Because the church has largely adopted a worldly system of dating, the walls of protection for our children which God designed have been broken down. We have provided our children with enough Christianity to ensure their guilt when they fornicate, but not enough to ensure their purity.

Our system of recreational dating has broken down; it is time to return to the biblical pattern for getting together. Apart from *biblical* dating or courting, there are many destructive consequences—emotional, sexual, and spiritual. But if a young man seeks to initiate a relationship, and takes full responsibility for the relationship under the woman's father, there is scriptural accountability and protection. It is the purpose of this small book to define, defend, and describe how biblical dating or courtship works.

Objections to this assessment of the modern dating system may tend to come rather easily. Why can we not point to the successes, the happy endings in the modern dating system? Besides, this whole thing seems to work on television. Three responses come to mind. First, it is certain that everyone with good will rejoice when a godly Christian couple dates, behaves themselves, and then marries. The success stories within the modern recreational dating system, *which certainly exist*, are not the problem with it. Nothing said in the following pages should be taken as directed against godly Christians who came together within the dating system. The criticism is directed against the system generally considered *as a system*. People survive plane crashes too, some of them without a scratch, and we should all be happy about it. But this acknowledgment does not disqualify us from opposing the general habit of crashing airplanes.

This relates to the second point. Generalizations are legitimate if they honestly describe an overall pattern. Generalizations are consequently *not* refuted through particular and individual counter examples. Honest Pharisees lived at the time of Christ, and they were not an embarrassment to Christ's scathing denunciations of their religious sect as a whole. Indeed one indication of a Pharisee's honesty would be his willingness to acknowledge the justice of Christ's sarcasm. Thus generalizations about recreational dating will not be universally true (they *are* generalizations). What we should ask from a generalization is whether it is honest and fair, not whether it is true in any given instance.

Third, "success stories" are not as abundant as may be assumed through briefly glancing around at church. Christians are not as open about their sexual behavior as pagans, and the tight lips can be deceiving. Our tendency is to judge based upon the outward appearance, and everybody at church sure *looks* moral. But many pastors in their premarital counseling go beyond such a cursory glance. Tragically, many pastors are now surprised when they find Christian couples who are behaving themselves sexually—"You *are*?" The *objective* data concerning unmarried Christian couples in the modern dating game is *not* heartening.

Our dating system, considered as a system, does not biblically prepare young men and women for marriage—at least for marriage as God designed it. A few basic reasons should at least introduce the subject addressed in this book. The modern dating system does not train young people to form *a* relationship. It trains them to form a *series* of relationships, and further trains them to harden themselves to the break-up of all but the current one. At the very least, this system is as much a preparation for divorce as it is for marriage. Whenever the other person starts to wear a little thin, you just slip out the back, Jack.

Further, the modern recreational dating system encourages emotional attachments apart from the protections of a covenant fence. This has been accurately called emotional promiscuity. A man and woman cannot function within a romantic relationship without becoming emotionally vulnerable to one another. Nothing is wrong with this vulnerability; it is just that we are delicate enough at this level to require protection before we enter into such as state, a protection which the Bible says is covenantal.

Moreover, the modern dating system also leaves the father of the young girl almost entirely out of the picture. The father, who ought to be protecting his daughter's sexual purity, sends her off into the dark with some highly-interested young man, and then does what he *thinks* is his job, which is to worry. "Well, dear," he says to his wife, "we can only pray. It has come to that." And he should worry, because the modern dating system *expects* a certain amount of physical involvement. True, the evangelical Christian version of this system allows only enough foreplay to get everybody concerned all messed up without any lawful release. We somehow think a godly Christian is one who can pre-heat the oven without cooking the roast.

Is there a better way? In the pages to come, we will address the underlying biblical principles involved in the pattern called biblical dating or courtship. In modern America, recreational dating is taken to be a positive good, like food, air, and sunshine, and is considered to be a necessary, inescapable activity. It is considered to be a normal and natural part of growing up—what could be more wholesomely *American* than taking a girl to the prom? It makes us think of the fifties, when things weren't so fouled up in our society. In reality, recreational dating is a custom which began in this century, and was entirely unknown at the time the Scriptures were given to us. This means that for those who take the biblical teaching on the family seriously, we should consider what the Bible has to say on the *formation* of families.

Men are created and called to initiate, and women are created and called to respond. But we are not mechanical robots—God does not want us to initiate foolishly, or respond foolishly. First, the Bible calls men and women to fulfill their respective roles in courtship, and secondly, they are called to fulfill them *with wisdom*. Such wisdom requires that we follow God's revealed design.

When people are taught that all single men and women are solitary agents, that the two sexes are exactly the same, and that they each approach a potential relationship in the same way, those who listen to this are going to get into trouble very quickly. This is because women are built to *respond*, and men are built to *initiate*. This is not just true at the beginning of the relationship during the courtship. Initiation and response provide a pattern a man and wife will follow throughout marriage until they die. This pattern of initiation and response is so deeply ingrained in us that a fence of protection is constantly necessary to guard against a foolish, instinctive use of it. That fence is called courtship; the absence of such a fence is typified in the modern dating system.

Women hate one thing more than having to initiate themselves, and that is when no one initiates. If there is a vacuum of leadership, women will be tempted to fill that void. This should not be mistaken for a feminine desire to initiate; they will be unhappy that they had to step into that role. This pattern of *fenced* initiation and response is clearly seen in the biblical pattern of authority and submission to a father prior to marriage, and to a husband through marriage.

Headship in marriage does *not* mean that women submit to men; it means *one* woman submits to *one* man. Her submission to her husband protects her from having to submit to other men. Prior to marriage, her submission to her father protects her from having to submit to other men. There is no overall biblical requirement that women be submissive to men in general. The biblical pattern is that a wife should respond to the initiative and leadership of her husband, and only to him. She is prepared and trained for this in her submission to her father.

If a woman were responsible to submit to men in general, her life would be unbearable—no one can serve two masters. But a woman who is responsive to a godly man is protected from having to submit to other men, most of whom are less than godly. She consequently has a great deal *more liberty* than a woman who is not protected in this way. Thus the so-called "independent" woman is not under any kind of protection. She is truly on her own, but with the result being that she is buffeted about by all sorts of men. But if her father were doing what he ought to do, or if she were in a marriage relationship where the husband was doing what he ought to do, she would be protected from the insults and harassment of men in general. This explains why some of the most "independent" women are so insecure, and why some of the most submissive women have a real security and strength of mind. Women inescapably need godly masculine protection against ungodly masculine harassment; women who refuse protection from their fathers and husbands must seek it from the police. But women who genuinely insist on "no masculine protection" are really women who tacitly agree on the propriety of rape. Whenever someone sets himself to go against God's design, horrible problems will always result. The Bible says that we find the way to true self-discovery through self-surrender. Those who exalt themselves are humbled, and vice versa. In the feminist movement over the last several decades, women have been looking for (and have not yet found) themselves. This is because they have been trying to find and identify their role apart from God's design. The beauty of biblical courtship is that *it never leaves women unprotected.*

Men are designed by God to initiate and lead, and women are designed to respond. In the formation of marriages, men are designed by God to initiate to the father of the woman who interests them. Women are designed to respond to an interesting suitor while in submission to their fathers.

For an example of such protection, if a man expects a woman to respond to something when he has not yet initiated, he is like someone who expects a tennis partner to return the serve when he has not yet served. This is an "easy way out"—young Christian men often abdicate in this way. They want to find out what the woman's response would be *if* they initiated—without actually having to take the risk of initiation. Once the man knows that the woman would respond positively, *then* he initiates. This is the coward's option, leaving the burden of the initiation on her. When the man abdicates in this way, the woman is being conned into taking the initiative. Having to deal with the girl's father prevents all this. This means that a man who is initiating in a relationship must take quite a risk in talking to her father. But God has designed it so that the man is the one who is to take such a risk. He initiates, and, if she has received her father's blessing, she responds. *This is biblical courtship.*

But before considering the biblical arguments which establish this as a pattern for courtship, we must first delay a moment in order to issue a few preliminary warnings.

The first has to do with the profoundly important distinction between *principles* and *methods*. Because our contemporary practice of recreational dating has failed so miserably, many Christians are hungry for alternative methods. "Just tell us what to *do!*" In this arena, as elsewhere, the Christian life is approached as though it were a paint-by-numbers kit. But nowhere is this kind of "connect the dots" thinking better calculated to bring disaster than in the realm of courtship. We are men and women with sons and daughters, not social engineers playing with interchangeable, interconnecting tinker toys. This simplistic but destructive mentality is revealed in questions like, "How many times must a young man come over before the young girl's father should allow him to sit next to her at the dinner table?" The author of this small book frankly confesses that the answer is none of his business, and that he doesn't really care. Seek to understand the principle, and appropriate methods will follow.

The second concern relates to terms. Already I have spoken of biblical courtship, and I have spoken of recreational dating. What do such terms mean? In a book like this, we must not only deal with the denotations of the terms, but also with the connotations. For some, the whole thing is quite simple. A *date* is when a young man and woman go out together on their own, and *courtship* is when a young man goes through the young woman's father. As far as this goes, fine. But what are the connotations? For some Christians, dating calls to mind a series of bad experiences in the back seat of a car somewhere, and for some others, it recalls a number of pleasant and happy memories leading up to a wonderful marriage. The term courtship is even more problematic. As more and more Christians respond to the problems created by our unbelieving culture's method for pairing off, they are adopting the pattern of "courtship." But they are also bringing in some extra-biblical connotations as they do so. For some, courtship means that we must all become retro-prairie muffins. The one being courted wears a gingham dress and bonnet, and the one courting rides his horse over from the Taylor Ranch after church on Sunday. And there they sit on the front porch swing, as Stevie Ray Vaughn mentioned earlier, "just a swangin'."

Others go even further back, with the phrase *courtship* making them think of Camelot and maidens in distress. This is actually a little closer to the origin of the word courtship. Courtship originally derives from the Latin *cohors*, from which we get *cohort*. It meant an enclosed yard, and included the retinue of men which would assemble in such a yard. Through obvious processes, we get words like *court*, *courtier*, and *curtsey*. We also get *courtesy*, which is behavior polished enough for court, and *courtesan*, a loose woman thought high-class enough to service the court. Courtship is related to the practice of medieval courtly love—the practice of waiting upon and serving a lady, seeking her favor. In the chivalric ideal, the lady in question was usually married to someone else. Courtship *as a term* has its etymological origin in a practice just as unbiblical as modern recreational dating. The one being "courted" was the woman, not her father. The one being "courted" was probably already married. Huh.

We live in a fallen world. One of the evidences of this is that we really have no adequate term to describe the way in which young Christian men and women should get together. Perhaps some time after Christians return to a more obedient practice, we will have been doing it long and well enough to be able to name whatever it is we are doing. In the meantime, we must use such terms as we have, hence, biblical courtship or biblical dating. We must reject the pattern of abdication, disobedience, and sexual immorality which we see all around us; hence, our rejection of recreational dating, or the modern dating system. But in doing this, we are bound to use whatever terms we select in a *qualified* sense. Some couples who "date" are in closer conformity with biblical principles than other couples who embrace the "courtship" model. So in this book I shall routinely refer to courtship, or biblical courtship, and sometimes to biblical dating. If a courting couple goes on a *date*, we should not all panic and relegate this horror to the same category as nation rising up against nation, or kingdom against kingdom. The end is not yet.

CHAPTER ONE

The Authority of Parents

Remembering Courtship

Courtship is of interest to everyone. Perhaps one reader may
be able to apply the biblical principles of courtship directly,
while another is interested on behalf of his children—or grandchildren. How men and women come together, how they
come to be married, how they enter into the marriage covenant is not a matter of indifference. Well begun is half done,
and we need to understand what the Bible teaches about the
beginning of our married relationships.

As Christians we have to understand what the Bible reveals about the formation and structure of the family. If we
turn to Scripture, we will learn it doesn't just reveal how the
structure of the family should function once it is in existence,
but also reveals how families are to *come* into existence. The
Bible provides guidance for us at this critical point.

In modern America, we get men and women together
through a system which we are calling recreational dating.
This is so prevalent in our culture that we think it has always
been everywhere. We think recreational dating is a positive
good, necessary for the development of normal young people,
and is somehow an inescapable activity. In reality, this system
of recreational dating is a practice which began in this century, was unheard of during the time the Bible was being writ-
ten, and was unknown throughout most of the history of our
culture.

This system where a guy takes an interest in a girl, asks her out and then decides whether or not he likes her (and, of course, she does the same with him) is not to be found in the Bible. Now of course this does not mean that it is automatically sinful or wrong. Automobiles and computers are not in the Scriptures either. There are a number of things that are not *named* in the Scripture, but this doesn't mean that the practices themselves are necessarily unbiblical.

So how should we approach this? A number of problems with our system of recreational dating will be revealed when we look at the Word closely. We must look at those things which the Bible *does* teach about the structure of the family. If we take the Bible's teaching about the structure of the family very seriously we should take with equal seriousness what the Word says about formation of families. In Scripture, how do new families come into existence in the first place?

As years go by, our children get bigger, they get older, and it isn't that long before they get big enough and old enough to be thinking about what they are going to do after they leave home. They start to think about whom they might marry. Even though many parents would like to put *that* thought out of their minds and say, "No, I'm not really ready," God still requires parents to be ready. He has not given parents thirty-two years to figure this out; in the normal pattern, He has given nineteen years, or twenty-two years. Further, it is not a good idea for parents to try to figure out what they will do after the process has already started. They and their children both need to understand these things well beforehand.

So what does the Bible teach?

The Status of Daughters
The Lord wants us to be *biblical* Christians as we think through this issue, and the Bible's teaching on the position of daughters should be the first area of our consideration. We will begin by addressing the status of daughters in a biblical family:

Or if a woman vows a vow to the Lord, and binds herself to some agreement while in her father's house in her youth, and her father hears her vow and the agreement which she has bound herself, and her father holds his peace then all her vows shall stand, and every agreement by which she has bound herself shall stand. But if her father overrules her on the day that he hears then none of the vows nor her agreements by which she has bound herself shall stand; and the Lord shall forgive her because her father overruled her. But if indeed she takes a husband, while bound by the vows or by a rash utterance from her lips by which she bound herself and her husband hears it and makes no response to her on the day that he hears then her vows shall stand. And her agreements by which she bound herself shall stand. But if her husband overrules her on the day that he hears it, he shall make void her vow which she vowed and what she uttered with her lips by which she had bound herself and the Lord will forgive her. But any vow of a widow or a divorced woman by which she has bound herself shall stand against her. If she vowed in her husband's house or bound herself by an agreement with an oath and her husband heard it and made no response to her and did not overrule her, then all her vows shall stand and every agreement by which she bound herself shall stand. But if her husband truly made them void on the day he heard them then whatever proceeded from her lips concerning her vows or concerning the agreement binding her it shall not stand; her husband has made them void and the Lord will forgive her. Every vow and every binding oath to afflict her soul her husband may confirm it or her husband may make it void. But if her husband makes no response whatever to her day to day then he confirms all her vows or all the agreements that bind her. He confirms them because he made no response to her on the day he heard them. But if he does make them void after he has heard them then he shall bear her guilt. These are the statutes which the Lord commanded Moses between a man and his wife and between a father and his daughter in her youth in her father's house (Num. 30:3–16).

In this passage, we have a father confirming vows that his daughter makes while she is living in his house. We also see a husband who confirms any vows that the wife makes while in his house. We also are given an understanding of how this authority *transfers*. If a young husband inherits a particular vow made by his new wife, on the day that he hears it, he may say, "No." If he hears of it and says nothing, or if he hears of it and thinks it is a good idea, then of course the vow stands. If he hears of the vow and says, "No," then the vow is nullified.

If he hears of it and says nothing, we see how the principle of abdication is illustrated in Scripture. If he hears it and says *nothing*, then by saying nothing *he ratifies* the vow. According to Scripture, then, a husband or father *cannot* "not act." A husband and a father *act* by not acting. A man in this situation cannot "go somewhere" else and say that the whole thing distresses him. He may not say, "I don't like the situation, I don't want to deal with the vow, I don't want to be troubled by these things." Such a refusal to act is very clearly labeled in Scripture *as an action*.

At bottom, the real issue is not the nature of the vow, although the context shows that this is a vow to the Lord. Because the woman has vowed that she is going to give an offering to the Lord of some nature, some might object and say that this passage is simply talking about ecclesiastical vows, or some sort of vow to the Lord directly. But we must reason here *a fortiori*. If a husband or father has the authority to nullify a vow made to *God*, how much more may he nullify a commitment to baby-sit?

For example, suppose a woman foolishly promises to watch a neighbor's kids for the next eighteen months or so, and then she comes home, kicks herself, and says, "What did I *do*?" When her husband hears of it, he is not bound by her words. He has the authority to say that the commitment was not yet settled; it had not yet been ratified. According to biblical law, he has the authority to say that his wife is not bound by her commitment. Until he hears of it and says, "Yes," or hears of it and says nothing, the commitment is not final.

Now if such authority rests with the father or the husband concerning a vow made *to the Lord*, how much more does it apply to other issues? And how much more will it apply to such things as a commitment a daughter might make to an interested suitor? A vow a woman makes to the Lord would be the most solemn and weighty of all vows. If her father or husband can set this kind of vow aside, then he certainly has authority to set aside other lesser vows.

Another application from this passage is the fact that there is no hint here of a period of "intermediate independence" for daughters. We sometimes assume that as girls grow up they are to be treated in the same fashion as sons. This is false—in Scripture, sons *leave* home, daughters are *given*. This is the scriptural pattern. A son leaves in order to take a wife, and establish a new home. A daughter is given to a young man who is establishing such a home. The idea that a girl can get to the age of eighteen or nineteen, and leave her father's house in order to be out on her own is not scriptural. She remains under the authority of her father—even if she is physically away from home—and then when she is given in marriage, she comes under the authority of her husband. This is the normal scriptural pattern.

But we also see in this passage (v. 9) that some women serve as independent heads of households. "But any vow of a widow or a divorced woman, by which she has bound herself, shall stand against her." We see the same principle in the New Testament. Lydia believed and she was baptized, and her household (Acts 16:15). Lydia is treated as the head of *her* household in the same way the Philippian jailer is treated as the head of *his* household. We do not know Lydia's precise status (*i.e.*, whether she was a widow or not), but we do know Scripture treats her as the head of her household. A divorced woman is certainly *permitted* to return to her father's house (Lev. 22:13), but Scripture does not require it.

We are taught that any vow of a widow or a divorced woman by which she has bound herself shall stand against her. Now an older woman, an independent widow or divorced woman, is not under her father's authority. According to the Bible, if such a woman is being courted, she may make her own decisions. "A wife is bound by law as long as her husband lives; but if her husband dies, she is at liberty to be married *to whom she wishes*, only in the Lord" (1 Cor. 7:39). Obviously, if a woman were widowed when she was fifty years old, and her father is now seventy-five, there is no scriptural obligation for her to move back into her father's house and come back under her father's authority. The Scriptures require no such thing. She is now the head of her own household, and that is as it should be. The same principle applies to a younger widow or divorcee.

However, this is quite a different matter than a young girl of eighteen, trying to strike out on her own. Such a young woman may not say that she doesn't need her father's authority, and that she does not yet have a husband's authority. Such "intermediate independence" is not the scriptural pattern.

As we examine Scripture, we see the common phrase "married and given in marriage." Sons marry, and daughters are given in marriage. For an example of this, consider Psalm 78:63. The purpose here is not to exposit the psalm, but simply to exhibit a common biblical expression. It says, "The fire consumed their young men, and their maidens were not *given* in marriage." In the course of another train of thought, this phrase simply displays the scriptural way of thinking about marriage. Sons marry, and daughters are given in marriage. Given by whom? As we have seen, the Bible teaches that *fathers* have authority over their unmarried daughters, just as husbands have authority over their wives. Moreover, there is a natural transition made from the authority of the father to the authority of the husband, as we can see in the phrase *given in marriage*. The authority of a father therefore clearly extends to a daughter's romantic interests.

Having been so uncautious as to use the word "romantic," we must digress for a moment. This whole area of men and women coming together has been a propaganda playground for modern sentimentalism for many years. We should not be surprised to see the biblical principle fulfilled that whenever anything is worshiped idolatrously, that thing is lost. The worship of sentiment is the destruction of sentiment. But the world does not see it that way. How many times have we been told, *ad nauseam*, in songs on the radio, in movies, in books, that a person's heart can only be given by that person? "Well, she loves him." Or, "He loves her." And of course, true love will always overcome all obstacles—and the central obstacle in modern love stories is the blind opposition of parents. The course of true love must overcome all obstacles, chief among which is "father as chowderhead." Again and again, we see the propaganda for this culture of youth worship, wherein it is assumed that what is innocent and immature has wisdom, and that what is old and mature in biblical terms has no wisdom at all.

Romance is believed to be "the thing" which ties a marriage together, and it is further thought that young people understand the dynamics of romance far better than their elders. Now the emotional attraction and attachment we have for one another *is* a gift from God. But romance has the same function as the curtains of a house—it cannot serve as the concrete poured for the foundation. What establishes the foundation for any godly marriage is *covenantal faithfulness* to the God who gives us marriage. He gave us the principles, the rules, the laws that govern marriage, and we serve God with a whole heart as we take these things to heart, and then treat our spouse obediently and lawfully with a good will, dependent entirely upon the grace of God in Christ. With the whole heart a man should ask what the Bible requires of him in his treatment of his wife. A wife must ask the same concerning the treatment of her husband. When Christians enter into the covenant of marriage this way, they are blessed with wonderful marriages. Not surprisingly, an obedient man and wife have strong emotional and romantic attachments to one another. But when romance is the *foundation*, the house does not take very long at all before it starts to crumble.

So the Bible teaches that a father has legitimate authority

over his daughter's romantic interests. She may be emotionally attracted to a suitor. It may also be spiritual, it may be sexual; it could be a combination of all of three. Regardless, the authority of the father extends over the romantic interests of his daughter.

In the book of Deuteronomy, we see this paternal authority expressly applied to a daughter's marriage:

> If any man takes a wife and goes into her and detests her and charges her with shameful conduct and brings a bad name on her and says, "I took this woman, and when I came to her I found she was not a virgin." Then the father and mother of the young woman shall take and bring out the evidence of the young woman's virginity to the elders of the city at the gate. And the young woman's father shall say to the elders, "I gave my daughter to this man as his wife and he detests her; now he has charged her with shameful conduct saying, 'I found your daughter was not a virgin,' and yet these are the evidences of my daughter's virginity." And they shall spread the cloth before the elders of the city. Then the elders of that city shall take that man and punish him. They shall fine him one hundred shekels of silver and give them to the father of the young woman, because he brought a bad name on a virgin of Israel. And she shall be his wife; he cannot divorce her all his days. But if the thing is true and evidences of virginity are not found for the young woman, then they shall bring out the young woman to the door of her father's house, and the men of her city shall stone her to death with stones, because she has done a disgraceful thing in Israel, to play the harlot in her father's house; so you shall put away the evil person from among you (Dt. 22:13–21).

Before applying this passage, a few other matters must be cleared away. Some will perhaps react—"This is Old Testament law! What about the woman caught in adultery brought to Christ in the gospel of John? Didn't Jesus change all of this? Let him without sin cast the first stone, and all that." Now the woman in John was caught in "the very act" of adultery, and under the Mosaic code this was a capital crime. She faced the death penalty, and so they brought her to Jesus to trap Him into a contradiction of the law. "What do *you* think, Jesus?" But according to the law, it was a capital crime *for whom?* The law clearly requires capital punishment for both parties—the man and the woman both. This woman was caught *in the very act of adultery*, but somehow she was caught in such a way that she was there by herself.

We see the very common double standard for men and women at work here. They caught *her* in the very act of adultery without catching the man. God's standard for sexual morality does not conform to man's standards—He has no such double standard. God expects *men* to be as sexually pure as he expects women to be. No double standard exists in God's law. If a woman was an adulteress she could be executed for it, and if a man were an adulterer he could be executed for it. So the double standard on the part of Christ's adversaries here is evident. They catch a woman committing adultery all by herself, and they bring *her* to be stoned!

When Jesus said that the one without sin should cast the first stone, He did not mean one who was sinless in every respect. This would be to set the whole law of Scripture upside down, with no possibility of justice anywhere. No elder in any church could exercise church discipline because each elder has sinned at some time before in his life. No civil magistrate could execute a serial murderer because the magistrate has had sin in his life at some prior point in time. Jesus is *not* teaching that if someone is sinful, he may not execute judgment. The Bible requires judgment, and it requires sinners to make such judgments.

The Bible *does* however teach that a judge may not condemn someone for doing what that judge is doing. For this reason, I believe Jesus is saying that one without the sin of *adultery* should cast the very first stone. And the text is very interesting at this point—it says that beginning with the *oldest*, the woman's accusers began to depart. The older men knew they had been trapped, and they began to leave. When

Jesus finally tells the woman that He does not condemn her, He is not saying it would have been wrong to condemn. He had the authority to condemn or not to condemn. It would not have been wrong to condemn her if she had in truth been caught in the act of adultery, and the biblical rules of evidence had been observed. If she had died under such circumstances, she would have gotten nothing more than what she deserved. What was being presented to Jesus, however, was nothing less than a miscarriage of justice, and Christ would have nothing to do with it. Consequently, it is not possible to set this famous passage over against the passage from Deuteronomy. This is not an area where there has been a change of teaching between the Old Testament and the New Testament. Christ was not changing the definition of justice in the transition from the old to the new; He was insisting that the constant definition of justice be scrupulously and justly applied.

So what does the passage in Deuteronomy require? First, we find that the elders of the city were not Victorians; they were not prudish. They were not fearful of investigating the evidences of the woman's virginity. In many cases, modern Christians do not act in a biblical fashion because they handle sexual matters too gingerly—either that, or with the openness of pagans. As biblical Christians we should strive to keep our definition of propriety in line with that of Scripture. Secondly, we find out that this was not a law which required the woman to be executed because of her sexual immorality. To repeat, this is *not* a case of execution for sexual immorality.

In the Bible, *adultery*—sexual immorality in violation of an existing marriage covenant—is a capital crime. But in most situations, sexual behavior outside of a marriage betrothal or covenant was not a capital crime. The reason for the death penalty in the passage cited above was because of the sexual fraud involved. A man has married a woman believing her to be a virgin. He finds out, or comes to suspect, that she was not a virgin when they married, and he consequently makes this charge against her. Now it was a very serious charge indeed. If the charge was sustained, she was to be executed.

And if the charge was not sustained, he was to be fined and was not permitted ever to divorce this woman. He was required to provide for her because he was guilty of defaming her name.

If the woman was guilty of immorality, the problem which required execution was the fraud. Virginity was a priceless inheritance for the young woman to bring into the marriage. Now if the woman was not a virgin, and the man to whom she was betrothed *knew* this about her, and still married her, then this law did not apply at all. But if he thought she was a virgin, and he valued that highly (as he ought to have), and then came to find out she was not a virgin, then the law applied.

In the New Testament, we can see the parallel with Joseph's dilemma over Mary. He had believed (rightly) that she was a virgin. But when she turned up pregnant, Joseph knew that he was not the father, which meant that someone else had to be. He therefore assumed that she had to have been unfaithful to him. Since the Jews were under Roman authority at that time, this law from Deuteronomy could not be followed because the Romans would not have permitted it. Therefore Joseph, being a righteous man, tried to resolve the matter by divorcing her quietly. Joseph was mistaken about the facts of the case (for which he may be excused), but the Bible nowhere hints that he was wrong for wanting to put Mary away. Quite the reverse—he is described as a righteous man in the midst of his deliberations.

So in Deuteronomy, the law addresses a case of sexual fraud—*i.e.*, a misrepresentation is being made. Now the crucial ramification involves what it says if the charges made by the jealous husband were sustained. If the charges were true, and this woman had played the harlot in Israel, then the men of the city were to bring her out and stone her. The important thing to note is that they do this *in front of her father's house*. They do not execute her at a state penitentiary in the middle of the night. They execute her in front of her father's house.

Now why *there*? The biblical answer is that the *father* is responsible for the sexual purity of his daughter. When he gave his daughter to her husband to marry, he presented her as a virgin. But he had not lived up to his responsibilities; he had not taken care of his daughter the way he ought to have. Virginity was a priceless inheritance to be brought into the marriage; in this case the fraud consisted of falsely claiming to have that inheritance. For such fraud, the woman was executed in front of her father's house.

In Exodus 22:16–17, we see again that sexual immorality was not a capital crime in Israel, and again we see the role and responsibility of the father.

> And if a man entices a virgin who is not betrothed, and lies with her, he shall surely pay the bride-price for her to be his wife. *If her father* utterly refuses *to give her to him*, he shall pay money according to the bride-price of virgins.

In other words, if a man seduced a virgin then he was required to pay the bride-price, and could be required to marry her. The only possible requirement here fell upon the seducer. The father, however, was *not* required to give his daughter in marriage to this person. If the father utterly refused to give his daughter to him, the seducer was still required to pay money according to the bride price of virgins.

Now who determines whether or not this happens? The text is very clear—the father. The father of the daughter—not the daughter, not the seducer, not true love, not Hollywood—decides. Mundane old Dad makes the decision. Now obviously the daughter had seen something in this young man. But the father may not have seen it, or perhaps he did see it, but had a different opinion of it.

A common error among Christians holds that if the sexual act is completed, then the couple are married "in God's sight." Many destructive complications occur in contemporary culture because we have adopted the idea that people can be married in God's sight without being married. It is hard to say where this idea originated, but it has caused a lot of damage. If a couple marries and get divorced illegitimately, many Christians assume the two are "still married in God's sight." The biblical response is "No, they are divorced in God's sight"— that is their sin. They ought to be married. Even though they have no scriptural authority to be divorced, this does not mean that there is a transcendent invisible married state outside of the world.

We can also see the havoc this assumption can create when we consider it combined with the ramifications of immorality. We think that the essence of marriage is a sexual commitment. So when a man entices a virgin and he sleeps with her, we believe there is an obligation to marry. But this is true only on one side. An obligation may be placed on the man in question by the girl's father. Such an obligation *may* be placed on him but it need not be placed on him. Marriage is scripturally defined as a sexual relationship within the boundaries of a covenant commitment that has been formally ratified. The sexual relationship by itself does not constitute marriage.

When Paul talks about the problem of sacred prostitution in Corinth, he refers to Genesis where it says that a man will leave his father and mother and be joined to his wife and the two shall become one flesh (1 Cor. 6:16). Paul teaches that a man becomes one flesh with a prostitute just as he becomes one flesh with his wife. But this does not make the prostitute his wife. The thing that constitutes a marriage is a ratified covenant around a sexual relationship. *If the covenant is not there the marriage is not there.* If the sexual relationship is not there the marriage is not there.

Marriage is a public covenantal act. So if a man entices a virgin and lies with her he must pay the bride-price for her to become his wife. And if her father utterly refuses to give her to him, he pays anyway. The father has the authority to refuse to allow the public act of marriage—whatever the couple may have done in private.

Now if the father has the authority to say *no* when there is an *existing* sexual relationship, then how much more does the father have the authority to say *no* when there is nothing more than mild emotional or sexual interest? If he may say *no* when a couple has gone ten miles down the road, then how much more may he say *no* if they have gone fifty yards?

Conclusion

We have seen what the Bible says about the authority of fathers over their daughter's commitments. In Numbers 30, the *normal* pattern was for a woman to be under her father's authority until she came under her husband's authority. There are exceptions—widows or divorced women—who are the heads over their own households. We noted Lydia, who was the head of her household. But the modern pattern of an "interim independence" between father and husband was unknown. The idea that a young girl could say, "I'm eighteen and I can do what I want" would have been alien to the biblical way of thinking. In other words, the father has *legitimate* biblical authority over his young daughter's interests.

This authority is assumed in the common biblical phrase "given in marriage." This giving was not a token practice, as it is in modern weddings. It was a genuine gift, offered with genuine authority (Ps. 78:63; cf. Luke 20:34, Matt. 24:38). We only have a vestige of this understanding in our modern wedding ceremony. ("Who gives this woman to marry this man?") But in biblical times, this was far more than an empty tradition. The daughters were really given in marriage.

We must remember the biblical teaching on the authority of fathers with regard to their daughter's commitments. For this, we may recall Numbers 30:3–16, with particular notice paid to verse 5. "But if her father overrules her on the day that he hears, then none of her vows nor her agreements by which she has bound herself shall stand; and the Lord will release her, because her father overruled her" (Num. 30:5). As this passage shows, the normal pattern in the biblical family was for a woman to be under her father's authority until she came under her husband's authority.

Some may argue that the requirement in Numbers refers

only to a religious vow—a vow before the Lord. But if a father could nullify a vow made to God, how much more would he have the authority to nullify a promise made to a young suitor? But we do not *need* to rely on an *a fortiori* argument—the Bible acknowledges the authority of the father in a situation that directly relates to the subject of marriage—"If a man entices a virgin who is not betrothed, and lies with her, he shall surely pay the bride-price for her to be his wife. If her father utterly refuses to give her to him, he shall pay money according to the bride-price of virgins" (Ex. 22:16–17). This demonstrates that a father has legitimate authority in the area of his daughter's romantic interests. In this situation, there has been a failure in the home—the daughter was not brought up to resist seducers effectively—but the father's authority is still not set aside because of it.

In Deuteronomy 22:13–21, we saw that a father was held directly responsible for his daughter's sexual purity. When a man charged his bride with sexual fraud, the parents defended themselves against the slander by producing proofs of the daughter's virginity. If the charge was true, then the bride was executed *in front of her father's house*. This was not death for fornication, but rather death for sexual fraud. Virginity was an inheritance, brought into the marriage, protected and insured by the father.

"Therefore a man shall *leave* his father and mother and be *joined* to his wife, and they shall become one flesh" (Gen. 2:24). A son is reared up for independence. He is trained to leave, while still respecting his parents' godly counsel. A daughter is brought up to be transferred from one state of dependence to another. Sons *leave*, daughters are *given*.

In biblical courtship, the practical, *involved* authority of the father over the process is fully recognized and *appreciated*. With recreational dating, the authority of the father is treated as a vestige of another era, or as a joke. The task before us here is consequently for fathers to begin thinking of themselves in a biblical way. The disrespect that children have for their fathers in this area is really just an echo of the disrespect that fathers have of their own office.

In biblical courtship, the sexual purity of the daughter is protected and guaranteed by her father. He is her permanent chaperon, assigned to that office by God. With recreational dating, some degree of sexual activity is expected so long as they don't "go all the way," and those responsible for holding the line are the couples themselves—which usually means that the woman is the one who bears the brunt of the responsibility. She is expected to say *no* if she wants the erotic proceedings to stop, while he is commonly expected to get whatever he can.

With biblical courtship, the courting activity is publicly connected to the life of the family, most likely the family of the young daughter. With recreational dating, the privacy of the couple is paramount.

Virginity is an inheritance to be brought into a marriage, and the father of the bride is responsible to preserve that inheritance. But although virginity is important, if someone squanders that inheritance, the Bible does not require death—this is clearly seen in the earlier case from Exodus when a maiden was seduced. She was not put to death; the seducer was required to marry her if her father permitted it.

The pattern is different for sons. From the beginning, God has intended that sons leave home in order to establish a new home (Gen. 2:24). But when we remember the authority of the father of the bride, we see that when a young man leaves home, he does not become autonomous. He needs to approach the father of the young woman he seeks to marry.

CHAPTER TWO

Preparing Sons for Courtship

In the first chapter, we established the important scriptural principle that courtship directly involves the parents, especially the father of the woman. Parents have true authority as their daughters marry. Yet even when this authority is understood and accepted, a host of practical questions arises. It is not enough to understand the principle—the principle must also be *applied*. Application is where authority is seen, and the authority of parents is consequently very real in the area of courtship. Parents are not superfluous—they have true authority in matters of the heart. But as we come the issue of how sons are prepared for marriage, we see a difference in application.

The Bible teaches that sons leave their parents—"Therefore a man shall *leave* his father and mother and be joined to his wife, and they shall become one flesh" (Gen. 2:24). This means that, in contrast to the on-going protection provided for daughters, a son must be instructed thoroughly *before* he has left home.

The preparation of sons must therefore be done before the process of courtship has actually begun. If a daughter is in her father's house, and a young man comes and requests permission to start spending time with the daughter, her father can say that his daughter is not yet ready. He can continue to exercise authority over her until he sees that she is ready to be given in marriage. But a father must be anticipating his son's preparation for leaving, and be equipping him to go *be-*

fore that time comes. A son must be thoroughly instructed before he leaves home.

In Genesis 2, we have a very clear statement of God's pattern for the extended family. The Bible does not contain any warrant for patriarchal tribes as a governing *family unit.* The pattern for a man in the Bible is for him to grow up, leave his parents, and cleave to his wife. The wife, having been given in marriage, has transferred her allegiance from her father to her husband. Before this time, she had given submission to her father. If he was a wise father, she was brought up in such a way that she was able to transfer her allegiance to her new husband. Parents must be equipping their children to do this, with careful regard being paid to the difference between sons and daughters.

Of course this pattern is so deeply ingrained by God in our created nature that it is going to happen in some fashion whether we equip our children or not. Grown children will do this anyway, but if untaught, they will do it *badly,* and the parents are going to handle their leaving badly. When they leave, the parents should not wonder, "What went wrong?" The answer is that nothing has gone wrong—they were *supposed* to go. A father should want his daughter to *want* to leave when the right man comes for her. Fathers should want their daughters to want to transfer their allegiance to their new husbands.

Before they leave to take a wife, sons must be instructed in certain key areas. The first is what the Bible teaches about marriage itself. This means instruction in God's law concerning marriage—what does the Bible teach about marrying unbelievers? Cousins? The principles found in such passages as 1 Corinthians 6–7, Leviticus 18, and Mark 6:18 should be taught and lived out in the home. A son should be thoroughly instructed from the Bible on the nature and doctrine of marriage.

God defines what constitutes a marriage. His Word is the unalterable law concerning marriage. When John the Baptist came to Herod, he told him that it was not *lawful* for Herod to have his brother's wife. The problem was that Herod had stolen her, and then married her. But God's Word is our authority on marriage—not our hearts, not the law of the land, and not the practice of the king. What happens when homosexual "marriages" start to be recognized by our civil authorities? The Bible teaches that such rebellious legislation by a magistrate cannot change what God has declared a "perversion" into a "marriage." This applies to more than homosexual unions. The same principle would apply to a marriage between a brother and sister—God's law forbids it. This means it is possible to have *heterosexual* "marriages" that are outside the boundaries of God's Word. God's Word teaches that a man cannot have his brother's wife as Herod did. It is therefore crucial that our sons be taught the definition, meaning and purpose of marriage.

Sons must be taught 1 Corinthians 7:39— "a wife is bound by law as long as her husband lives, but if her husband dies, she is at liberty to be married to whom she wishes, only in the Lord." A basic principle is seen here, which is that a Christian must marry a Christian. Believers don't have the authority even to *think* about marrying a non-Christian. So what happens if one does marry a non-Christian? Is it a real marriage? The answer is *yes*, but why is it different than the other situations mentioned above? The answer is found in what the *Bible* teaches about these marriages. The Bible says true marriages can be entered disobediently, while other forms of disobedience do not result in a marriage at all, but rather in perversions. There is a difference between a disobedient marriage, and a disobedience which pretends to be a marriage. Even if the particular prohibitions of Scripture do not apply to them, it is extremely helpful for sons to understand what the Bible teaches about the boundaries of marriage. It helps to establish in their minds that *God is the Lord of marriage.*

Scripture shows us that marriage is a covenantal union, and *not* a metaphysical union. Marriage is an earthly relationship, an earthly covenant, surrounded by biblical protections which God has set up for us. If someone violates the terms of that covenant, if he has made a solemn vow and then was not faithful to it, then he has broken the covenant. Jesus directly addresses this in His teaching on the subject of divorce; He permits divorce and remarriage on grounds of sexual uncleanness. In a similar way, Paul deals with "mixed marriages," and what to do when an unbeliever deserts a believer. If the unbeliever leaves, the believer should let him go, she is not bound in such circumstances. She is free to remarry.

A son should know what constitutes the formation of a marriage, the obligations of a marriage, the boundaries of marriage, and what conditions apply to a lawful dissolution of marriage. It is remarkable how people get married all the time and nobody ever thinks about asking them for a definition of what they mean by it. If someone were to say, "I am going to Europe," he usually could answer questions about where Europe is, and so forth. Yet many get married without even knowing what marriage is. If someone joins the Navy without knowing what a navy is, then that person is a fool. A young man therefore should not approach the married state without a clear concept of *what it is in the sight of God*. If he does not know, then he is a fool, and his parents are fools, because they have not taught him what a married man *is*, and what God requires of him as a married man.

He should also be taught what the atmosphere of married life was intended by God to be. The best thing godly parents can do here is provide their children with several decades of viewing consistent Christian living within a marriage—in the home in which they were born. The value of this is inestimable. The Bible teaches that we learn by *imitation* (1 Cor. 4:16; 11:1). Paul calls upon Christians to imitate him as he imitates Christ. We find a similar teaching in Ephesians 5:1, where it says we are to be followers, *imitators*, as children of God and we are to walk in love. Children learn by imitation. At birth, all of our children enroll in an 18–20 year course entitled, "How to Treat a Husband or Wife." How father and mother speak to one another is constantly being soaked up by the children. Of course, this does not mean children are stuck with every bad lesson they were ever taught. We know and acknowledge that all parents are sinners. No parent is a perfect example, but even when parents sin, they may still provide a good example of how to humbly confess and acknowledge the wrong. Neither is God restricted by massive disobedience on the part of parents. God's grace is larger than even this; He can graciously intervene in the life of someone who grew up with thoroughly disobedient parents. But we must never sin that grace may abound. It is always an incalculable blessing for children to grow up in such a way that they know "in their bones" how to speak lovingly to a wife and respectfully to a husband. When someone asks them why they live the way they do, they are surprised. "This is normal, isn't it?"

I was blessed enough to grow up in a home where I never heard my parents raise their voices to each other—eighteen years of calm graciousness. When children grow up in a home like this, what *single* lesson can we say is learned? This is not *one* lesson, it is an attitude, an atmosphere for the home. The home should be the place where there is this aroma of godliness *all the time*. As fathers speak to their wives, they are training their sons to speak to *their* wives. This is a great opportunity to teach sons how to be married, from the inside out. How many sons who grew up in pagan homes can see Christian marriages only from a distance? They can hear sermons and read books on the subject—and God does work through such means—but this doesn't teach all the intangible nuances of the godly home. Children in a believing home have free and constant access to this wonderful means of instruction.

So the first thing to teach a son is what a godly marriage *is*, the second is to teach what godly married life is *like*. Another important issue is that of masculinity. Sons must be taught biblical masculinity. The Bible teaches that in the marriage relationship, the initiative, the headship, is to be with the male. This is seen in courtship, and carries over into the marriage relationship itself. One aspiring to be a head must not act in courtship as though he were aspiring to be a foot. This means that a son must be equipped and taught to *lead* a woman. A husband must be willing to be the head of the woman as "Christ is head of the church."

As parents consider their little boys who appear to have a surplus of this initiative, a surplus of masculinity, they may err by leaving it entirely undisciplined, or they may seek to discipline the troublesome masculinity *out*. Of course, aggressive masculine boys can produce all types of interesting disciplinary situations. As parents teach and discipline, they should not seek to squelch this, but rather to direct it into godly channels.

For example, it is very easy for adults who see a boy who doesn't know what he is talking about, but who acts like he does, to hammer him in order to get him to shut up and learn a little humility. But boys must be trained to take risks, which means being confident in the midst of the unknown. As they do this on an immature level, fathers should work with them, and teach them, without destroying the masculine impetus.

Courtship reveals how necessary this masculinity is. Many modern young men approach a girl, and they are quite serious as far as *their* intentions go, but they are afraid of interfering with *her* life. "You know, she is going to graduate soon, but she wants to go to school at Notre Dame, and I don't really want to go to Notre Dame, and showing interest in her would really disrupt all her plans." But the whole *point* of courtship is to disrupt a young lady's plans. A godly young woman is not going to stand around waiting for marriage. Rather, she will be preparing herself for marriage. This means she will be heading in some particular direction, and not just marking time. A young man should not be afraid of disrupting, because marriage is by its very nature a disruption of her previous way of life. But there are many guys who have an "excuse me for existing" kind of attitude—which is not very masculine—when it comes to a potentially serious relationship with a young woman. This kind of apologetic, hand-wringing "masculinity" is not what parents should want to instill in their sons. A son must not be afraid to take the initiative in such matters.

The young woman might not want her life to be disrupted by him, but this means her problem is not with the disruption in itself, but rather with the particular young man. In such a case, her father needs to tell the young man, "No." This can be an unsettling prospect for anyone, and this is why boys should be brought up to be tough enough to take such treatment. Instilling this toughness is very important. Men will get knocked down in the course of their lives; they should learn how to take it when they are boys.

A son should also be taught the centrality of fatherhood in the godly home. One of the key ways a son may be protected from sexual immorality is through instruction from the Word of God. For an example of this parental instruction, we can consider the fifth chapter of Proverbs:

> My son, pay attention to my wisdom; lend your ear to my understanding, that you may preserve discretion, and that your lips may keep knowledge. For the lips of an immoral woman drip honey, and her mouth is smoother than oil; but in the end she is bitter as wormwood, sharp as a two-edged sword. Her feet go down to death, her steps lay hold of hell. . . . Drink water from your own cistern, and running water from your own well. Should your fountains be dispersed abroad, streams of water in the streets? Let them be only your own, and not for strangers with you. Let your fountain be blessed, and rejoice with the wife of your youth. As a loving deer and a graceful doe, let her breasts satisfy you at all times; and always be enraptured with her love. For why should you, my son, be enraptured by an immoral woman, and be embraced in the arms of a seductress? (Prov. 5:1–5,15–20).

When a son is instructed by a father who is a consistent Christian and godly father, the very thought of fathering a child outside the protections of the marriage covenant will be enough to make him almost physically ill. A son should be taught that the sexual hunger he has is a gift from God—*and* that he doesn't get to eat for several more years. This requires the inculcation of self-control, but parents do not have to wait until their son is in the grip of sexual temptation before they may instruct him on how to respond to it.

There are many *other* areas requiring self-control where this virtue can be acquired and made habitual from the time their son is a small boy. In Proverbs 5:15–20, what is the context of this teaching? In verse 1, a father says that his *son* must pay attention to his wisdom. This is not teaching from one Christian man to another; it is from a father to a son. He teaches his son to stay away from loose women who will destroy his soul. The son is not even to think about it. But a father may only teach self-control successfully if he has established a pattern of teaching self-control over the years.

Many parents try to teach their sons about sexual self-control after sexual temptation becomes an issue. But sexual self-control is just one species of the genus "self-control." Sexual self-control is simply a subset of self-control. Parents should be inculcating self-control first, throughout the son's life. When a young boy starts whining, and tries to demand something, and the parents say, "No," they are teaching self-control. This becomes a habit established in his character long before adolescence arrives. When sexual temptation first arrives, the necessary response of self-denial must not be an entirely new concept. If parents indulge a little boy's emotions, his whims and his tantrums, then what is going to happen to that young man when he becomes consumed with sexual desire? He is going to vanish like straw in fire. Why should a young boy, who never said *no* to any of his passions, suddenly start saying *no* to this incredibly strong passion after he has grown to be a man? Parents who dream this way are guilty of wishful thinking.

Another important way fathers can protect their sons from sexual immorality, and prepare them for sexual fidelity in marriage, is through demonstrating the importance of *fatherhood*. An example from my childhood illustrates the point

very well. One time—I must have been in junior high school—
I remember a young boy at the bus stop bragging about his
father's sexual exploits. His father had been in the South Pacific during the Second World War, and this boy was greatly
pleased with how many half-brothers and sisters he must have,
scattered all across the South Pacific. His father had been very
immoral, and had apparently been bragging to his son about
it. This kind of sentiment can be very appealing to a non-
Christian (male) mind, and the young boy no doubt thought
he would get to behave in the same way. As noted earlier, if a
son has been taught properly, if a godly example of fatherhood has been lived out in front of him, if he consequently
has a high view of marriage, and a high and respectful view of
women, the thought of fathering a child out of wedlock should
be enough to make him almost physically ill. "Do you mean
there is a child out there that *I* fathered, who is growing up
without a covenanted father?" The thought should be enough
to turn his stomach. But this will only happen if he has seen
what marriage *ought* to be like. He should have an exception-
ally high view of children, the married state, and what it means
to be a husband and a father. He should be sickened by the
thought of sexual activity outside of marriage because it leads
to children outside of covenant protection. No Christian
young man, having been properly taught, and having seen the
right example, will have anything to do with the propagation
of bastards.

Lastly, a father should teach his son that in the modern
world, *gentlemen* are sorely needed. A common problem in
the way many modern men seek to initiate a relationship can
be illustrated in how they place the burden on the women. In
courtship, a woman's fundamental protection is provided by
her father. But this does not mean that her suitor has no responsibility to act like a gentleman. Suppose the father has
given his permission for a young man to court his daughter.
As a godly man approaches a woman, he should assume *all* the
risk. For one example, he should not beat her over the head
with the "will of God"—her name is not "Suzy Lordschoice."

He should not tell her what *God* wants for her life. He is not a prophet. James sternly forbids us to act as though we know what the future holds—

> Come now, you who say, "Today or tomorrow we will go to such and such a city, spend a year there, buy and sell, and make a profit"; whereas you do not know what will happen tomorrow. For what is your life? It is even a vapor that appears for a little time and then vanishes away. Instead you ought to say, "If the Lord wills, we shall live and do this or that." But now you boast in your arrogance. All such boasting is evil (James 4:13–16).

A young suitor has absolutely no business telling a young lady that he has "prayed about it," and that the Lord wants her to marry him. He should be acting on what he believes to be the will of God for *him*; the will of God is not a "club" to be used on her. The man should be telling her what he would like to do, and what, Lord willing, he will do. He must not tell her what God told her to do. It is a cowardly way to place the burden on the woman, and in addition James identifies all such presumption as evil.

Our lives are a mist. We should believe ourselves to be walking in the will of God, but we understand this by faith, not by sight. We have no idea whether God will have us doing the same thing tomorrow that we are doing today. Lord willing, we will be doing the same. If we are not, He is the Lord. When a young man proposes marriage, he does not know if it is the Lord's will for them to get married—they might both get hit by a truck the week before the wedding. He should simply trust that he is in the will of God as he asks her to marry him, and should also, as a gentleman, not try to strongarm her into an agreement through forceful appeals to the "will of God."

If, for any reason, she says *no*, he should never press her for her reasons. She owes him *no* explanation. Neither should he protect himself by seeking to find out her sentiments *first* before he expresses his intentions. Of course, protection against unpleasant surprises is one value of going through the father first. But regardless, where there is any pressure to be felt, it should be assumed by the young man.

Sons therefore need to be trained to be gentlemen. Gentlemen are not wimps; they take responsibility for others. We have seen that, in the courtship process, the fundamental protection is provided by her father. But if the father is wise, he will only admit a suitor who is the kind of man willing to be the young woman's *second* line of protection. A young man is acting in a cowardly way if he says something like, "Well, I have been thinking about us—what do you think about us?" He has not said what he was thinking about, and wants to find out her thoughts first. He doesn't like taking risks, which means he is not acting in a masculine way. A son should be brought up to assume as much of the risk as he can.

The fact that a suitor must approach the father first means many of these problems will not develop at all, or will happen to a much smaller extent than they do in the course of recreational dating. There are "lines" that work on girls that don't work that well on their fathers because the fathers have good memories.

"I *remember* that line, and I know what you are up to young man."

CHAPTER THREE

Preparing Daughters for Courtship

We have established the authority of the parents in the process of courtship, and we have addressed how parents are to undertake the preparation of their sons. We come now to the preparation of daughters for courtship. For obvious reasons, this is very important. If a daughter is not cooperative, the practice of courtship *will not work*.

Trust is at the center of all family life. Trust is what makes authority bearable. Now we have seen the principle that parental authority does not stop at the perimeters of a child's heart. Children are under their parents' authority in the matter of courtship; this is particularly true for daughters during courtship. We have also seen in the Scripture how sons *leave*, and daughters are *given*. A man will leave his father and mother, and seek the hand of a young woman from her father. He approaches him and asks permission for the privilege of approaching his daughter. The father will grant or withhold that permission. Obviously, if he is a godly father he will never make such decisions arbitrarily, or capriciously, or without consulting his wife and daughter.

In order for a daughter to rejoice in her submission to her parents in this matter, she obviously has to trust them. This trust must be built up over the years *in the little things*. A father who is capricious or dictatorial in the little things cannot expect a natural and unfeigned submission from his daughter on a matter of this importance. We have to recognize that establishing this pattern of behavior is not something which can be done just by snapping the fingers. It has to be established over many years.

Paul insists that Christian fathers be reasonable men. "Fathers, do not provoke your children, lest they become discouraged" (Col. 3:21). This passage provides a general injunction for fathers. It does not say what the children might become discouraged *about*—it simply provides a general word to fathers. Now suppose a father, who is bringing up his young daughter, neglects this biblical admonition. Or, to put it another way, suppose he disobeys Paul and is in sin. His children become discouraged because, for example, he constantly sets them up for difficulties, criticizing them in an ungodly way. After seventeen years of this, his daughter is turning into a very lovely young lady (at least on the outside), and the guys are starting to come around. She then has the misfortune of having her father buy a copy of this book, and he starts to talk about how he should take responsibility over all this courtship business. His daughter is thinking, "Oh, great. He ruins my life, and now he wants to wreck my one ticket out of here!"

Officious overbearing fatherhood is a recipe for disaster. If fathers are not building trust in their daughters *from the time they are little*, established through love, care, compassion, and sternness when necessary, then the daughter is going to be very hesitant about trusting her father in such an important matter. We like to deceive ourselves, thinking we can be selfish in the little things because our children are little, but that when something really important comes along, we will rise to the occasion and do the selfless thing. This is a self-flattering lie. Parents must prepare themselves to do the right thing in the great things by doing the right thing in the small things. The word Paul gives here is particularly addressed to *fathers*. If a man is habitually selfish in the little things as a father, then he is going to be selfish in the big things. If his children grow up seeing him be selfish, and then he starts to exercise authority in matters like courtship, they will be nervous *at least*. How could they not be?

The Bible teaches that we reap what we sow. We thank God for His mercy—we certainly do not reap *everything* we have sown. But because God has spared us in many different situations, the temptation is to start presuming upon God's grace and think that we have a "right" to have Him bail us out of all our follies. We do not want to have to pay the consequences for a disobedient, discouraging treatment of our daughters. The Bible teaches that this is a vain hope.

A young woman who is brought up properly will hear this teaching about courtship and be *relieved*. She doesn't have to fight guys off all by herself. But she can only be relieved if she has the kind of father who has done good to her consistently over the years, *and she knows it*. This is the kind of pattern that fathers must live out in order to establish their "courtship credentials."

In Scripture, it remains true that if a man has not been an obedient father, this does not remove his paternal authority. He may be a poor father, but he remains a father. So even if a man has been disobedient, this does not grant his daughter the right to disregard anything he says. The point being made here is that a man is simply making life difficult for himself and his daughter if he doesn't treat her right all her life. There should be loving trust between father and daughter. She should know that when it comes to a matter of this importance, she will not have some "selfish" thing foisted upon her. Her father would never approve of something without constantly keeping her best interests in mind. She knows he will not be selfish in the big things because she knows he has not been selfish in the little things.

With this in mind, what sort of direction and preparation may parents provide for their daughters?

Modesty and Prudishness

The Bible very clearly requires modesty in Christian women. As the reader may have noticed from time to time, there is a direct relationship between *how* a woman dresses, and whether or not men come around—and, of course, there is another connection to what *kind* of men come around. It is important for parents to note that modesty excludes two practices, which are unfortunately common today even among Christians.

The Bible teaches that women should be covered up, and not too tightly either (Matt. 5:28). The temptation to lust varies between sons and daughters. The boys want to notice, and the girls want to *be* noticed. Neither sex should be indulged in this.

Men respond visually to women. Suppose a young man sees a girl on the street, turns about face, and chases her down to meet her. What is he responding to? The greatness of her soul? The brilliance of her mind? The sweetness and gentleness of her spirit? Of course not—he is responding to how she *looks*. Now there is nothing wrong with this in itself, or with women seeking to be beautiful and attractive. But there is a profound difference between seeking to be *attractive* and trying to be *seductive*.

Fathers are responsible for the modesty of their daughters. It was mentioned earlier in this book that a certain kind of "relationship problem" is not really a relationship problem. If a guy simply talks to a girl and imagines that she likes him, and he builds up this intense relationship in his head, then he has a personal problem. In the same way, if an attractive woman is "lusted after," that is the man's problem. The Bible does not require pretty girls to wear paper bags over their heads to keep from stumbling all the brethren.

It is also very clear that women can do certain things that will entice that wrong kind of gaze, and encourage men to respond in an impure way. Simply put, a girl should be "covered up." She should not dress in such a way that a godly man has to duck down alleys or climb trees to get away from her. If he has to look at the ceiling whenever he is talking to her, a godly young man he should be thinking, "Where is her *father*? Why did her father let her go out like this?"

The answer is that her father let her go out like that because her father abdicated his responsibility. The principle is

very simple; if girls dress immodestly they will attract the
wrong kind of attention. Boys like to desire and girls like to
be desired. Fathers must teach their daughters self-control
through loving them into a secure relationship which excludes
any tendency to exhibition. In addition, godly mothers will
teach their daughters the techniques of modesty.

Oftentimes a Christian father is more reticent to talk
about these things than the world is. He doesn't want to say
no to his daughter for fear of making her think that he has a
dirty mind. And he doesn't really want to explain to his daughter that fifty percent of the world is going to notice what he
noticed, and he does not want to tell her exactly *what* that
fifty percent will be thinking. She may pretend she doesn't
know, but of course, she knows deep down what kind of reaction it is going to cause. She may not have thought it through,
but it is the reaction she wants, a fleshly reaction. She must
learn not to indulge it. Related to this, her father must not
allow her to indulge it. A father must not hope that when she
is married her husband will put his foot down. Or that maybe
the new dress code at the local Christian school will do the
trick. He must not hope that someone *else* will address it.
Fathers may not walk away from their responsibility in this.

Secondly, women should not be decked out in an ostentatious way (1 Pet. 3:3). They should not think they have a
right to strut their stuff in the mall (Is. 3:16–26). In short, a
virgin daughter should be taught to dress in a way consistent
with an honest man's honest approach of her *father*. If her
manner of dress is seductive, not attractive, then any man
who is attracted to it will *not* be trying to find her father.

In the context of 1 Peter 3:3, we see an apostle's instruction to married women, but the teaching also applies to single
women as well. The way young women behave when they are
virgins also affects the way they will behave when they are
married. Peter says that women are not to let their "beauty"
be a matter of outward adornment. Now modern Christians
like to overreact to any references to this apostolic teaching,
and accuse those who refer to it as desiring to institute a neo-

Amish regime of ugly clothes. Matters are further compli-
cated by those believers who *do* think the apostle is enjoining
plainness for women. As with so many issues, the balance is
found in between.

We have to understand the history and culture of the first
century. Women in the Roman world used to really "crank up
the volume" in their personal appearance. The problem addressed by Peter is *not* hair-arrangements in themselves, or
perfidy of pony-tails. No, Peter is directing his attention to
women who were ostentatious, making a display of themselves.
The women of that day would braid jewels into their hair, and
then sprinkle it with gold dust. Peter is saying that Christian
women are not to display themselves in such an immodest
way.

Some Christians hold, through a misunderstanding of this
passage, that "it is a sin to wear make-up." Peter *is* teaching
that it is a sin for a woman to look like she fell face-down into
her make-up, or like she puts it on with a trowel. "Do not let
your beauty be that of arranging of hair, or putting on gold, or
of wearing fine apparel, but let it be. . . ."

The point is that women should seek to be beautiful by a
certain means, through the hidden person of the heart. This is
not the Christian equivalent of "she has a nice personality."
Sarah is the example Peter gives. As she obeyed Abraham,
calling him her lord, Christian women are to seek to be her
daughters as they do good. Sarah was *externally* a very beautiful woman, even in her old age, but her beauty originated
from within and worked its way out. In the same way, a man's
daughters should be taught to cultivate an inner beauty of a
gentle and quiet spirit. Peace should pervade a young woman's
demeanor. There should be an absence of anxiety, so that the
inner calm will work its way out. And such calm daughters
will be beautiful on the outside.

In our society, women are repeatedly told *ad nauseam*, by
those periodic packaged lies called women's magazines, that
it is their responsibility to deck themselves out in such a way
that they "keep" their man. A woman may be able to do this

successfully in her twenties, and then have to work a little harder in her thirties and forties. *Then*, if she still buys all this foolishness, she really has to work in her fifties and sixties, because she is *always* competing with twenty-year-olds. If a wife treats fidelity in marriage as a prize to be obtained through competition, then somewhere, sometime, she is going to lose. This is the way of the world. But if she approaches it as a Christian woman, the older she gets, the more beautiful and serene she gets (1 Pet. 3:5). This means that fathers who are preparing their daughters to be given in marriage should not let their daughters display themselves in an ostentatious way.

Consider what Isaiah thought of the daughters of Zion who liked to display their wares at the mall. God does not think much of external beauty when that is all there is. If beauty is limited to just the outer crust, the result is incongruous. As Proverbs comments, a beautiful woman without discretion is like a gold ring in a pig's snout. The two do not go together. A woman who is externally attractive without gentleness of soul is scripturally obnoxious.

> Moreover the Lord says: "Because the daughters of Zion are haughty, and walk with outstretched necks and wanton eyes, walking and mincing as they go, making a jingling with their feet, therefore the Lord will strike with a scab the crown of the head of the daughters of Zion, and the Lord will uncover their secret parts." In that day the Lord will take away the finery: the jingling anklets, the scarves, and the crescents; the pendants, the bracelets, and the veils; the headdresses, the leg ornaments, and the headbands; the perfume boxes, the charms, and the rings; the nose jewels, the festal apparel, and the mantles; the outer garments, the purses, and the mirrors; the fine linen, the turbans, and the robes. And so it shall be: Instead of a sweet smell there will be a stench; instead of a sash, a rope; instead of well-set hair, baldness; instead of a rich robe, a girding of sackcloth; and branding instead of beauty (Is. 3:16–24).

The prophet Isaiah apparently did not have a very high view of the supermodels of his day, or of the women who wanted to be just like them. Of *course*, the issue is not the lawfulness of a bracelet, or a scarf. *The issue is attitude.* God hates pride and arrogance, which certainly *can* be manifested through ankle jewelry, and various other acoutrements. A brief walk through the shopping centers of America will show how dedicated we are to making women beautiful in this way —on the outside only. The issue is not whether it is permissible for women to dress nicely. But is *idolatrous* attention being paid to it? God threatened judgment on Israel for this kind of cosmetic arrogance and pride, displayed in the streets of ancient Israel. Christian fathers, therefore, should not let their virgin daughters act like they are not virgins, or as though they don't want to be virgins.

If a daughter dresses in such a way that sexual attention is going to come to *her*, then it is seductive and wrong. She should be dressed in such a way that anyone who is attracted to her could consistently and honestly come to *her father* and tell him about his desire. If she is dressed *modestly* and a young man comes onto her in the wrong way, then he cannot speak with her father honestly. And if the father knows what is going on, will not permit him to have anything to do with her. He will want a suitor who is attracted, but whose attraction is godly and honest.

Our culture acts as though sex is everything; sexual permissiveness is one of our great gods. Our modern pagans see sex in everything until a Christian sees it the same way. Then the pagan response is, "That's the problem with you Christians. You see sex in everything." We must ignore such double standards because our only standard is the Word of God. When a father lets his daughter go out in public, he is responsible for how she appears, and he must be willing to answer for how she looks, and what kind of men she attracts. If she is consistently attracting the "wrong kind of man," it is because her father is "the wrong kind of father."

Christians are not naive; we know that we are sexual beings, and that we are *always* sexual beings. That which distinguishes Christianity from the world is not a lack of awareness of the presence of our sexuality in everything. Rather, Christians understand the constant *presence* of God's covenant law governing any application of our sexuality. Consequently, we handle the courting relationship very gingerly—not because it is dirty—but because it is potent.

The world mocks us, and says we are afraid of sex. But look around at our culture and consider whether we are right in being fearful of the destructive power of sex whenever it is unleashed apart from God's covenant protections. These covenant protections are in large measure protections of *women*. C.S. Lewis commented once that "a society in which conjugal infidelity is tolerated must always be, in the long run, a society adverse to women." This is very true—our culture hates and despises women, despite all the feminist rhetoric to the contrary. And when a society hates women, it is a paramount duty of fathers to protect their wives and daughters.

A father has no obligation to protect his daughter from sex—if he attempts such a thing, he is disobeying God. The issue is morality, and not prudishness. It is false and unbiblical for courtship to be treated as though it were entirely a "spiritual thing." The courting relationship should be handled carefully by Christians because it is a volatile *sexual* relationship. The fact that it is unconsummated does not keep it from being sexual. When a young man approaches a girl's father, there is no sense anyone pretending that something platonic or spiritual is happening. "Mr. Smith, may I have your permission to speak with your daughter about missions?" The young couple is out having dinner at a restaurant, not in the third heaven. The sexual relationship is *there*, like an unfired pistol—loaded and cocked. A godly young man who comes to a girl's father is seeking a sexual relationship with that man's daughter. The fact that he goes to the father does not mean he must pretend that the sexual attractiveness of the daughter has nothing to do with it. It simply means he is seeking an honest sexual relationship in an honorable and biblical way.

On the Other Hand

The Bible is very clear in requiring fathers to protect their daughters. The Scripture is equally clear in saying that feminine duties include modesty and an avoidance of ostentatious display. Because this is so clear, many conservative Christians have emphasized this teaching *alone*, at the expense of everything the Bible says. It is obvious to us that when a girl goes out with an unbuttoned blouse, her father is leaving her unprotected. It is less obvious that if she reacts *against* her femininity, and dresses in overalls all the time, she is equally unprotected, although in a different area.

The Bible has a very high view of the importance of feminine beauty. It is mentioned often; it is praised highly. Moreover, the sexual aspect of it is not hidden away or neglected. This understanding is also something which fathers should take care to inculcate in their homes.

There are three areas which should be mentioned. The first concerns the fact of feminine beauty, the second concerns the biblical warrant for a cosmetic augmentation of feminine beauty, and the last area concerns the sexual element. All of this should be held in balance with the earlier discussion of Peter's admonition, as well as Paul's expressed concern: "In like manner also, that the women adorn themselves in modest apparel, with propriety and moderation, not with braided hair or gold or pearls or costly clothing, but, which is proper for women professing godliness, with good works" (1 Tim. 2:9–10).

First, the Bible recognizes and approves of the clear fact of feminine beauty—it is assumed to be a part of God's creation. The patriarch Abraham married a beautiful woman. "Indeed I know that you are a woman of beautiful countenance" (Gen. 12:11). When Abraham got to Egypt, it was clear that the Egyptians shared his opinion of her (Gen.12:14). A taste for beautiful women apparently ran in the family, because Isaac also married a beautiful woman. "Now the young woman was *very beautiful to behold*, a virgin" (Gen. 24:16). Jacob followed the practice of his father and grandfather, when he loved and married Rachel. "Rachel was beautiful of *form* and *appearance*" (Gen. 29:17). For various reasons, we react against such plain biblical statements. One reason is that we live in an egalitarian age, and to say that one woman is very beautiful implies that another woman may be less so. The implication is sound; the error is in the egalitarian assumption that there is something unfair about this.

The other concern might come from more conservative and prudish Christians, who are embarrassed that the Bible records the fact that Rachel was built like a brick house. "That's not very . . . well, biblical." But actually, the *Bible* sets the standard of what is biblical and what is not. The author of Genesis does not just say that she was pretty from the neck up; he tells us that her *form* was beautiful. This will be discussed at greater length below, but Christian modesty does not require a woman to look like a boy.

Abigail was a wonderful combination of beauty and intelligence (1 Sam. 25:3). Esther was a beautiful woman (Esther 2:7) who replaced Queen Vashti, another beautiful woman (Esther 1:11). Job's daughters were compared in their beauty to all the other daughters of the land, and the Bible tells us that they were more beautiful (Job 42:15). The beauty of the bride in the Song of Solomon was great enough to strike her husband with awe (Song 6:4). Throughout the Bible, we see feminine beauty described and praised. Clearly, there is nothing wrong with the daughters of the Christian church seeking to be beautiful as well. This is part of God's creation order.

Cosmetics are also are part of His design. Some, taking the passages cited above, have erroneously concluded that make-up is sinful, and for a young woman to adorn herself artificially is vanity. As discussed above, there is a point when a woman is relying on her cosmetics and jewelry in a sinful way. But that point is *not* the point at which she puts them on.

The Lord describes His adornment of His covenant bride Israel in this way. Obviously the example would be a poor one if God was doing for His bride what was unlawful for a man to do for his.

And when I passed by you and saw you struggling in your
own blood, I said to you in your blood, "Live!" Yes, I said to
you in your blood, "Live!" I made you thrive like a plant in
the field; and you grew, matured, and became very beautiful. Your breasts were formed, your hair grew, but you
were naked and bare. When I passed by you again and
looked upon you, indeed your time was the time of love;
so I spread My wing over you and covered your nakedness.
Yes, I swore an oath to you and entered into a covenant
with you, and you became Mine," says the Lord God. "Then
I washed you in water; yes, I thoroughly washed off your
blood, and I anointed you with oil. I clothed you in embroidered cloth and gave you sandals of badger skin; I
clothed you with fine linen and covered you with silk. I
adorned you with ornaments, put bracelets on your wrists,
and a chain on your neck. And I put a jewel in your nose,
earrings in your ears, and a beautiful crown on your head.
Thus you were adorned with gold and silver, and your clothing was of fine linen, silk, and embroidered cloth. You ate
pastry of fine flour, honey, and oil. You were exceedingly
beautiful, and succeeded to royalty. Your fame went out
among the nations because of your beauty, for it was perfect through My splendor which I had bestowed on you,"
says the Lord God (Eze. 16:6–14).

In this passage, the Lord God adorned His bride. He provided her with baths, with oil, with embroidered clothes, with
badger-skin sandals, linen and silk, bracelets, a necklace, nose
jewelry, earrings, and a crown. These are all gifts from God,
and are treated very differently from the proud and haughty
wearing of finery described by Isaiah. Throughout Scripture,
the practice of feminine adornment through jewelry is assumed
and practiced. When internal beauty is forgotten, and women
begin to adorn themselves externally *alone*, and begin to rely
on the outside *alone*, the results are, biblically speaking, ugly.
But when a woman fears God, and adorns herself for her husband, the practice is praised. When Abraham's servant first
found Rebekah, he gave her a nose ring (Gen. 24:47). Later,
he gave her "jewelry of silver, jewelry of gold, and clothing"

(Gen. 24:53). The bride in the Song of Songs adorns herself with perfume. "How fair is your love, my sister, my spouse! How much better than wine is your love, and the scent of your perfumes than all spices" (4:10).

The practice of young women adorning themselves was so common among God's people that it is used easily as a passing comparison. When Isaiah prophesies a great blessing for God's people, he puts it this way: "Lift up your eyes, look around and see; all these gather together and come to you. As I live,'" says the Lord, "You shall surely clothe yourselves with them all as an ornament, and bind them on you as a bride does" (Is. 49:18). Salvation is glorious; salvation is wonderful; salvation is like *jewelry*. "I will greatly rejoice in the Lord, my soul shall be joyful in my God; for He has clothed me with the garments of salvation, He has covered me with the robe of righteousness, as a bridegroom decks himself with ornaments, and as a bride adorns herself with her jewels" (Is. 61:10). Jeremiah asks, "Can a virgin forget her ornaments, or a bride her attire? Yet my people have forgotten Me days without number" (Jer. 2:32). To forget the Lord is compared to something a bride would never do—forget or lose her bridal ornaments. In Old Covenant and New, brides are adorned, and they provide a wonderful picture of God's gracious salvation of His people. "Then I, John, saw the holy city, New Jerusalem, coming down out of heaven from God, prepared as *a bride adorned* for her husband" (Rev. 21:2). In short, the belief which some Christians have that jewelry, make-up, perfumes, good clothes, *etc.* are somehow necessarily worldly is entirely mistaken. As fathers set the standards for their households, they must be careful to require balance in their daughters. No biblical requirement exists which requires Christian girls to dress in mattress covers; at the same time, a blank check is not given to mimic the various forms of the world's ostentatious display.

The last aspect of this will perhaps be more problematic to some parents. The Bible requires sexual modesty and decorum from the daughters of biblical families. Yet this is not a requirement that women pretend they are something other than a woman—or that *men* pretend the women are something else. The requirement of modesty is not a requirement of *asexuality*.

In Israel, when a girl had matured into one capable of lovemaking, she was considered marriageable. In the passage from Ezekiel, quoted earlier, when the Lord looked upon Israel and saw that her time was the "time of love," the Hebrew word *dodim* indicates that she was ready for sexual lovemaking. As a little girl grew into a young virgin, her sexual readiness was not a dark secret. In the Song of Songs, the brothers of the Shulamite (typical brothers) did not believe she was ready for this—"We have a little sister, and she has no breasts. What shall we do for our sister in the day when she is spoken for?" (8:8) The Shulamite responds indignantly to their assessment, and says, "I am a wall, and my breasts like towers; then I became in his eyes as one who found peace" (8:10).

The balance is that a woman should be trained to be modest, and not flaunt her body, or display it in a lewd manner. At the same time, she should never be made to feel as though it is a sin to be shaped like a woman. The Christian definition of feminine modesty collides equally with the wantonness of the world, and with the restrictiveness of, for example, the Islamic faith.

Paternal Protection

As a father protects his daughters, he must realize that the way he appears to them is different from the way he appears to his sons. He is setting an example for his sons to *imitate*. They want to be like their father, learn from their father, treat their wife like their father treats their mother. A son is imitating how his father behaves. But a daughter is not using her father as a standard to imitate, but rather looking to him as a pattern or standard to hold up against a potential husband. She is not going to be like her father; she should want to marry someone who is *like* her father. A father should be able to say, in good conscience, "I don't want you to even think about a man unless you respect him as you respect me." This is not an unreasonable standard; God has created daughters to respond favorably to this. Daughters are designed readily to honor and respect another man more than their father—but it must be the right kind of man. A father does not set this standard to ensure that she gets no man. Rather, he is ensuring that she will get a good man, a man who will take care of her.

When the Bible says wives are to honor their husbands, it is also telling virgin daughters what they should be preparing to do. Fathers need to set up a pattern of loving their wives so that their sons can be trained in how to love a woman, and daughters can know what is reasonable to expect from a godly man. Because daughters identify love with security, how the father treats their mother, and how he treats his daughters, is very important. If a young daughter is not being loved biblically, the result is insecurity. And insecurity leaves a daughter with poor sexual defenses.

Our culture tells us so many lies about men and women that it is hard to know where to begin unraveling them. One central lie is that women who are immoral are interested in sex in the same way that men are. This is simply false. Immoral men have a problem with self-control over a fleshly appetite. Immoral women are usually desperate for the security of a lasting relationship; they are sometimes so desperate that they try anything. Now of course women can have their hearts hardened like anyone else. The adulterous woman in Proverbs can wipe her mouth and say, "I have done nothing wrong." Women can become so hardened that they do become like men in their approach to sexual relations. In the first chapter of Romans, Paul says that "even the women" can get to this point of sexual depravity.

So how can the father protect his daughter? First, he should teach her to honor her father and mother so that she will know how to honor and respect her husband when she marries. Secondly, her father should love her tangibly. He must communicate that love and security—show it so that she understands it, receives it, and takes it in, in such a way that it becomes a part of her permanent frame of mind. She must not be left hungry for masculine attention. Fathers who leave their daughters hungry in this way are asking for trouble when it comes to the inevitable attentions of young men.

I remember a conversation my parents had in the car one time when I was a small boy, concerning a visit to some acquaintances of theirs. This family had a very young girl, and on the way home my father commented to my mother that the parents were going to have problems with her relations with men as soon as she was old enough. Years later, that is exactly what happened. But how did he know this? He, a relative stranger to her, noticed that this little girl, when he sat down in their home, was all over him, hungry for attention. When a little girl is not getting the attention from her father that she needs, she remains hungry for male attention and she will seek it elsewhere. Now when a little girl does this with someone she does not know, she is usually a pain in the neck. But what happens when this young girl, still hungry for male attention, suddenly matures and becomes sexually attractive? She still has the same hunger she has had for many years. She is now sexually desirable, but her interest in relationships with men is not a sexual interest. She is hungry for the security her father did not provide for her. This hard story has been repeated over and over again. Now of course, hard stories do not provide grounds for setting aside God's law. A lack of love and attention from a father cannot, and does not, justify immorality on the part of the daughter.

Nevertheless, God's law applies to other areas besides our sexual attachments. Included is the prohibition of stumbling others, daughters included. Fathers may not leave their daughters unprotected in this way. Fathers must give security; the daughter must be protected, and she has to know it. When she meets a man she respects and honors, the father does not have to worry about her being too attached to him to leave. God has built her in such a way that she wants to be given *by* a godly man *to* a godly man. She wants to be married, and she wants to transfer her allegiance to her new household.

Godly Responses

There are four basic situations for which a Christian girl needs to be equipped. If she has been brought up well, she will combine in her demeanor a gentleness of spirit—ready to respond to a godly suitor—with a firm and articulate ability to send someone packing. We can start with the easiest situations.

First, daughters need to know how to deal with strangers. This means Christian girls need to learn a godly rudeness. In a corrupt culture such as ours, this ability is increasingly necessary. If she has been taught well she will learn to incorporate into her demeanor a gentleness of spirit, which will result in Christian beauty, along with a firm and articulate ability to say *no* in all appropriate ways. If the daughter is at all attractive, she will need to learn a holy rudeness. Pagans will stop her on the street, and ask her to come to a wet T-shirt contest. Men may sexually proposition her. "Will you sleep with me?" Young Christian women need to know how to respond bluntly. In certain situations, to be polite is to compromise the faith.

Many Christian women have been taught that to be rude is, well . . . rude. But when the glory of God is at stake, as well as *the honor of a Christian virgin*, Christian girls need to learn how to be rude. This ability to react strongly is going to be increasingly necessary as our culture deteriorates further. When the angels visited Lot in Sodom, his house was soon surrounded by sodomites who wanted some action. We are not far away from this attitude which regards sexual attractiveness anywhere as some sort of public property.

A number of years ago, during the Iran/Contra controversy, a certain small incident in the midst of the larger controversy revealed the fact that we already have the mentality of Sodom. Perhaps the reader might recall that Oliver North's secretary was named Fawn Hall, and she was a very attractive woman who became a public figure on account of the political fracas. One of the mainstream pornographic magazines requested that she take off her clothes and pose for them. Our society has gotten to the point where, if someone is sexually attractive, it is assumed that there is a "right" to demand sexual favors. In a culture such as this, Christian women have to be prepared (in the name of the Lord, to the glory of God) to tell inquiring men to get lost, and immediately after, to drop dead.

Second, Christian girls need to be taught how to "create distance" with casual acquaintances. Daughters and parents need to avoid naivete about friendly acquaintances, whether at church, school, youth group, *etc.* Christian girls need to know how to create "distance" with acquaintances *without* rudeness. A young woman should not assume that just because he "hasn't asked me out" or he "hasn't talked to Dad," this means he is not interested. If he comes around a lot, if he "happens" to be there frequently, if he shows up at every Bible study she attends, then it is best to assume that he is interested. Mild flirtatiousness can be pleasant and appear to be non-threatening in group situations, but it is extremely unwise. In social settings with various acquaintances, a young woman needs to know how to be warm, friendly and *distant*. This demeanor is something which she should learn from her father and mother.

Third, a young daughter should know what to do with men who approach her openly and honorably—men who request dates. Suppose he comes and says, "May I take you out?" The daughter should be prepared to say, "You will have to talk to my father." In this way her father is acknowledged *by her* to be her authority in this. If the young man then comes to the father, the father should be non-committal until he has had a chance to talk with his daughter about the suitor. He will tell her what he thinks of the young man, and ask her what she thinks.

It is not always feasible to have the young man speak with the father first. The young man may not know about the standard of courtship this family has, he may not know who her father is, *etc.* The important thing is that the authority of the father is represented by her in any conversation with potential suitors. That authority should be understood by the suitor right away. Handled properly, this is a tremendous relief to the daughter. If the father has always shown her that he seeks her welfare under the authority of God's Word, then she can rest secure. This is a *security* for her because she knows her father will protect her.

Lastly, it is important to acknowledge that a young man who approaches her father first—someone who is "doing it right" does not thereby gain any necessary advantage. Talking to a young woman's father is not the same thing as staking a claim, or establishing dibbies. Just because he learns the procedures of courtship does not mean that he is the right man for her. Parents have to be careful to guard against the suitor who says, "In this church they emphasize courtship, so that means I have to butter up the parents." Virtually every community contains young people who manage to be popular with the elders, and who are equally obnoxious to their peers. Such young men are a real hazard in the practice of courtship. Parents need to be prayerful, wise in the Word, and *nosy* about a young man's background, life, lifestyle, relationship to peers, *etc.* Parents are not vulnerable to the flattery that is commonly given to young girls, but they *are* vulnerable to a different kind of flattery. They must not be taken in by manipulation. They should not grant any request easily.

The subject of courtship should be a regular topic of conversation around the dinner table as the family talks and visits together. Parents should not hide what they think about the young men and women in their Christian community. Parents should never be like Isaac and Rebekah, who were in grief of mind over Esau's wives, but did not tell him until *later* (Gen. 26:34–35; 28:8–9).

Many times, young people do not get wisdom from their parents because they are not prepared for the teasing grief they think they will get from siblings. Parents should be careful to discipline for destructive teasing. Such teasing has to be kept well within bounds—it is very dangerous to keep any child from discussing possible courtship interests with the family.

At all times, fathers should know that the way they train their daughters will culminate in how they give them away at the wedding.

CHAPTER FOUR

The Culmination of Courtship

We have now come to the point where we should tie together some of the final details concerning scriptural courtship. We should consider first the criteria for courtship, some miscellaneous details about courtship, and then lastly, the governmental issues raised in the godly formation of families.

By what standard should a future spouse be chosen? How do we understand who would be a good match for our daughter? If a son asks for advice on courting a young woman, on what basis would the advice be given? Our situation would not be very much improved if we were to go from a system based upon a young girl "liking" a guy to a system based upon her parents "liking" a guy—from the system of "recreational dating" to a pattern of courtship based upon parental prejudice and whim. Such decisions are very important, and cannot be left to *anyone's* current whims. The following discussion is phrased according to the standards the parents of the daughter should have, but they apply equally to the earlier discussion concerning sons.

The decision about a future spouse will affect the happiness of the children, grandchildren, and great-grandchildren. It is a very important decision. But because it brings with it a host of unknown variables, we cannot base the decision on our knowledge of all the details in the future. We cannot make our decision based on what *we* predict might happen twenty years from now. Rather, we must proceed on what God has revealed in his Word. God *does* know the future so we must obey Him. When we obey the principles and laws He sets forth, we can then trust Him for the results. We know that He is sovereign over all the unknown variables, and He requires us to submit to what He says in His Word. Not only does He not require us to ascertain our own fortunes, He forbids it.

So the first principle is that all Christian courtship must occur *in the Lord*. "A wife is bound by law as long as her husband lives; but if her husband dies, she is at liberty to be married to whom she wishes, *only in the Lord*" (1 Cor. 7:39). This text concerns a woman previously married, but we can clearly see the general principle Paul is invoking here—when it comes to the marriage covenant, believers must not be unequally yoked with unbelievers.

Paul is talking in this passage about what a woman is to do when her husband dies. We can see Paul's application of a general rule to a particular situation. The general rule is "you shall not be unequally yoked." This applies not only to marriage but to *anything which yokes*. Christians should not be tied to someone who is uninterested in doing things "God's way." An unequal yoke sets Christians up for disobedience and compromise. Consequently, God prohibits it.

In this application, Paul says a wife is bound by law as long as her husband lives, but if he dies she can marry whom she wishes—only in the Lord. If a woman has been married for twenty years, and her husband dies, then who is her "head" now? The Bible is clear that she is free to marry whom she wishes; she does not have to go back under her father's authority. But if the husband is alive, biblical marriage law assumes that he is the head of the household, whether he wants to be or not. If a woman does not have her husband and she has children, then she is the head.

Paul applies the general principle to the specific question created by a widow who wishes to remarry. The principle is to marry "only in the Lord," and to not be unequally yoked. The same principle applies to young people who have never been married. This means that godly parents should teach their children they must court and marry "only in the Lord."

The objection might be raised that "the Bible says you can't marry an unbeliever, but it doesn't say you can't date one." This is quite correct because the Bible doesn't talk about "dating" *anyone*—Christian or not. Here is our problem: in the modern world, dating is seen as a romantic/sexual activity that is legitimately detached from all covenant commitments, *i.e.*, there is no desire for a covenant yoke. Consequently many think there is no threat in dating, because dating is disconnected from any yoke. It is true that dating is not a yoke, but all romantic relationships between men and women *should* be yoked. If there is a yoke of courtship, then marriage is in view. And if marriage is in view, then courtship must be restricted only to believers. To argue that the Bible only prohibits marriage to an unbeliever but does not prohibit courtship of unbelievers is like arguing that the Bible prohibits murder but not attempted murder. Christians may only court Christians, and may only be courted by Christians.

But what is a Christian? We live in an apostate age, and the term *Christian* has been greatly debased. An unequal yoke can certainly be established between a genuine believer and a false professor. Many young women have lied to themselves at just this point. "Is he a Christian?" "Well, he goes to church with me." "We talk about God together." "He reads the Bible sometimes." Or, as my youngest daughter said once when we were joking about this problem, "He knows the story of Noah."

A young woman, under romantic pressure, may start to revise God's requirements in her head. If this begins to happen, her father must provide the cold water of obedience. If she really likes a man, she may begin to seriously question whether the way she was raised is totally correct. But she is not an objective, passive observer in this; she is changing her mind because she is being tempted, just like Eve. "Did God really say. . . ?" This is why it is so important for fathers to maintain their authority, so they can protect their daughters.

Parents should not be content with a son or daughter-in-

law who would go to heaven if he or she died. The Bible requires all believers to be likeminded. Consequently, our children must only court those who are *likeminded* (Phil. 1:1). If
all Christians are required to be likeminded, how much more
must a husband and wife be? To neglect this is to bring the
widespread disobedience of this command into the marriage
and home.

There are two aspects of this concerning which parents
should be aware. First, parents should look for likemindedness
in that which is *doctrinally* affirmed and understood. For example, should parents permit their daughters to be courted
by men who do not understand or accept the doctrine of the
sovereignty of God's grace? Of course not—an immense number of practical marital concerns are directly related to this
doctrine.

When Paul requires likemindedness, he is looking for
something which will "fulfill his joy." This requirement is
placed upon the entire church. We, as believers, look forward
to the time when God will have finished building His church
without spot or wrinkle, or any other blemish. This requirement of likemindedness will be fulfilled. But that great day is
not yet here, and Christians wrangle and disagree about many
things. If, however, we have failed miserably as Christians in
obeying the Lord at this point, we must repent and seek the
Lord's blessing as we pray and strive for likemindedness. We
must lament and confess our sin, and in every area where *we*
have any responsibility, we must insist upon likemindedness.
This has obvious application to the formation of new families.
As our children court, if God requires that "all Christians
everywhere be likeminded," *how much more* should a husband and wife be likeminded? This is especially true considering the fact that the wife must consider her husband her
head, and honor him as she honors Christ. Such doctrinal
questions affect how the children of this union will be edu-
cated, whether they will be brought up to serve and worship
God properly, whether they will be baptized as infants, and
so forth.

If a young couple has fundamental and deep doctrinal differences, the two are going to have serious problems in their marriage. Should a father who understands the majesty and sovereignty of God permit his daughter to be courted by a man who disputes the sovereignty of God? Of course not. Such matters are not abstract, dry theological controversies. They affect everything we do. When a young couple has a child who dies in the first year, how will the young husband comfort his wife? How can he, if he has a theology which says that God wanted to prevent this tragedy but couldn't?

This does not mean husband and wife must agree on everything in the Bible before they marry. Some things are revealed in Scripture to be less important than others. Further, some other disagreements are not a problem because the people involved are clearly on their way to further likemindedness. In other words, the existing disagreements are not permanent. Nevertheless, all such matters have to be conducted with great wisdom.

Likemindedness is also seen in what is *done*. A young man may share the parents' confession of faith (and that right gladly if the daughter is pretty enough), but still not *live* as though he believed it. Does he apply the Bible to every aspect of his life—work, education, politics, television, *etc.*? In other words, is he obedient? A man may not know as much as another man, but does he obey what he knows?

The Bible says we are to "adorn" our doctrine; we are to decorate what we believe. Many people say they believe something but do not live as though they do. Obedience is intimately connected with true likemindedness. Likemindedness is not just an intellectual exercise; it is an assent to the truth of God, embraced fully. Should parents want their daughter to be courted by someone who belongs to the same church or denomination but who doesn't put into practice what he says he believes? For example, does he *apply* his understanding of the sovereignty of God to all things—his work, what he does in leisure time, how he would educate his children? If he doesn't, then he should be disqualified on the basis of a lack of likemindedness.

A third principle from Scripture has to do with the financial stability and responsibility of the suitor. In our earlier discussion of seduction, we saw that a young man who seduced a girl could be forced to marry her, unless the girl's father forbade it. But in either case, whether he married her or not, the young man was required to pay what was called the bride-price. This mandatory bride-price is also seen in Deuteronomy 22:28–29:

> If a man finds a young woman who is a virgin, who is not betrothed, and he seizes her and lies with her, and they are found out, then the man who lay with her shall give to the young woman's father fifty shekels of silver, and she shall be his wife because he has humbled her; he shall not be permitted to divorce her all his days.

In cases of seduction and rape, such a bride-price was mandatory. This meant that the woman was an endowed wife, and in addition, she could not be divorced. In a biblical society, the price of immorality was high, *and fell on the man*. Fifty shekels of silver was a lot of money, and higher than the bride-prices which could be negotiated under normal circumstances.

This biblical system of bride-pricing meant that financial stability on the part of the suitor could be required, and provided economic protection for the woman. In unbelieving systems, the dowry is given by the bride's family to the groom; in a biblical society, the young man could be required to demonstrate his financial responsibility by giving a bride-price to the woman. In David's situation, Saul required him to demonstrate his military prowess in setting the bride-price for Michal at one hundred Philistine "scalps" (1 Sam. 18:25). The fact that Saul was being unreasonable in trying to get David killed does not change the fact that the bride-price was publicly set, and was negotiable. The burden of that bride-price was placed on the suitor.

Of course, the family of the bride was not required to *require* the bride-price. But in that society a young woman without such protection was a concubine, not a free endowed wife. The distinction between the two kinds of wives is clearly reflected and marked in Scripture. For example, a betrothed concubine was expected to be faithful to her future husband, but if she was not, the penalty was less than that for an endowed wife. "Whoever lies carnally with a woman who is betrothed as a concubine to another man, and who has not at all been redeemed nor given her freedom, for this there shall be scourging; but they shall not be put to death, because she was not free" (Lev. 19:20). For an endowed wife, whether betrothed or married, the penalty for infidelity was death.

In Exodus 21:7–11, we find more on the subject of the bride-price. In this situation, the case law perhaps indicates an intermediate status between that of an endowed wife and a concubine. In this situation, there was a bride-price, but the payment went to the family of the bride, and was not provided as a protection to the bride herself. Nevertheless, she still received a number of significant protections.

> And if a man sells his daughter to be a maidservant, she shall not go out as the menservants do. If she does not please her master, who has betrothed her to himself, then he shall let her be redeemed. He shall have no right to sell her to a foreign people, since he has dealt deceitfully with her. And if he has betrothed her to his son, he shall deal with her according to the custom of daughters. If he takes another wife, he shall not diminish her food, her clothing, and her marriage rights. And if he does not do these three for her, then she shall go out free, without paying money (Ex. 21:7–11).

Under normal circumstances, an endowed wife had "divorce insurance" in any money given her by her father, and in the money given to her in the bride-price paid by her future husband. But even when the money went to the family of the bride, as here, she was still protected by it. So the system of bride-pricing was *not* a system where women were bought and sold like cattle; the issue was the guaranteed financial protection of daughters. In contrast, in our society today, women are extremely vulnerable financially. When a man leaves his wife today, his standard of living typically goes up, while that of the deserted wife goes dramatically down. In a hard-headed biblical society, this would not be the case. We have learned the lessons of romanticism so thoroughly that we tend to ignore the obvious economic ramifications of modern marriage, treating them as "separate issues." In Scripture when they are not treated separately (because, to be frank, they are not), we rush to the conclusion that women had the status of chattel in biblical society. But in reality, women then had far more financial security than modern women.

The applications for Christian families today are not so obvious, however, but we can at least see that when a father of a young woman enquires into the financial stability of the suitor, he is not prying. The romantic propaganda of our day typically portrays all such concerns as mean-spirited and materialistic—everyone knows "all you need is love." But our rebellion against God's ways always bears fruit. The system of bride-pricing meant that a young man not only had to be *able* to support a wife, but he also had to put some money where his mouth was, and to prove that he could do so *up front*. As Christians grow and mature in their understanding of biblical ethics, we may see a return to the biblical perspective which seeks the privilege of endowing our daughters and future wives. Until then, we must not express amazement when our daughters are roughly handled because we provided them only with the protections which a previous era would have associated with concubinage.

A fourth biblical principle is that our daughters must only be courted by one they find sexually attractive. The Bible is very clear that marriage includes conjugal duties, and they are of such a nature that they should not be made burdensome through marriage to someone unattractive. "Do not deprive one another except with consent for a time. . ." (1 Cor. 7:3).

The biblical writers were not at all Victorian, and neither should we be. It would be more accurate to say that the biblical writers were *puritanical*, that is, they had a very high view of God's teaching on sexual morality. But this is not at all the same thing as sexual "prudishness." Prudishness can be defined as the desire to pretend that sex in marriage is not sexual, which is a lie from the enemy. Christian young people should court someone, or be courted by someone, whom they find to be sexually attractive, in a broad sense.

As discussed earlier, the two things that define a marriage are the sexual relationship and the marriage covenant. Sexual activity without a covenant is not a marriage, and a marriage ceremony without sexual activity is no marriage. Marriage is covenanted sex with attendant covenantal responsibilities. According to Paul, a man who goes to a prostitute is one flesh with her, but he is not married to her. What is a man's responsibility when he repents of such fornication? His clear and obvious responsibility is to walk away from it. A man has no responsibility to marry the last prostitute he was with. He must separate from the sin, and he must leave the one with whom he was sinning.

So marriage is a covenant made around the sexual relationship. God made us male and female, and intends for husband and wife to desire one another. Parents who love their children will not put them in the awkward situation of having to obey this requirement when it is a burdensome one. With a biblical mindset, a wedding is a time of joyful sexual tension. This should obviously be a factor during the time of courtship as well. The bride adorns herself to make herself beautiful, and the bridegroom rejoices over her beauty (Is. 61:10; 62:5). Obviously, as a wedding is conducted, and the marriage is consummated, the beauty of the bride is alluring to the bridegroom; it is sexual.

In summary, the Bible shows that those who engage in courtship should be fellow believers, they should be likeminded, pleasing in their mutual company, the man should be able to show that he will support the woman well, and they should both be pleased at the prospect of sleeping together.

In addition to such clear-cut biblical principles, there are other issues which fall under the heading of wisdom. Both the parents and the couple should consider things like cultural background, education and intelligence, calling, personality traits, *etc.* When it comes to such things, decisions should not be made impulsively.

When someone marries in disobedience to the clear requirements of Scripture, the elders of the church should be prepared to exercise church discipline. But there are many areas that are simply matters of wisdom; no direct scriptural teaching prohibits marriage between a man and woman with extremely diverse cultural backgrounds. At the same time, wise parents will take all such things into account. Parents should also consider sub-cultural backgrounds. Once the honeymoon is over, such things can become far more important than they were during courtship, and provide a constant source of friction for the young couple. Parents should be able to anticipate such problems.

To illustrate, levels of education and intelligence are important. A man is required to be the leader, and the woman is to respect him in that leadership. What if there is a disparity in their abilities that will make this difficult? There is also the question of calling. If he wants to be a missionary, is she ready for this? What about the compatibility of their respective personality traits? These things need to be thought through and worked out ahead of time.

As discussed earlier, another area which parents should evaluate is the young man's willingness and ability to take responsibility. This includes his ability to be disruptively masculine. Suppose John wants to marry Susan. But he knows that after she graduates, she is going to try to get a job in Seattle where her grandparents live. He goes to her father and says that he would ask her to marry him, but she has *other plans*. Now if John is really interested in Susan, and if he is masculine, he should cheerfully *want* to interfere with her plans. If she is not interested in marriage, she will not mind if he asks her father; there will be no imposition. Her father will just say *no*. If she is interested in him, it will not be an imposition either.

Women are not supposed to sit on the couch and wait for somebody to marry them. They should always seek to do something productive with their lives in the meantime. Consequently, men who are seeking a helper are going to have to seek this helpmate from among women who are going in other directions at the time. A man who understands masculinity and marriage should know generally what he wants to do, and he should be seeking a woman who agrees to *come with him*. It is not the other way around. He is not coming into her life in order to help her with her vocational calling. Of course if a husband loves his wife as Christ loves the church, he is going to help her in many ways. But the basic direction and orientation of their lives should not involve him surrendering everything God has called him to do for her sake. The Bible teaches that the woman was made for the man, not man for the woman (1 Cor. 11:9). A man and a woman in marriage are therefore to be oriented to one another differently.

Parents of the young lady should be aware of three kinds of men: men who are confident in a godly way, non-Christians who are confident in an ungodly way, and Christians and non-Christians alike who are insecure, and who lack a masculine confidence. Arrogant confidence is something that God prohibits, but in the minds of many women this is mistakenly thought to be better than no confidence at all. Even though he will mistreat her, it demonstrates at least *some* kind of masculine strength. When men fall away from the Lord, they do so for all kinds of reasons—money, career, a woman, sex, drugs, alcohol, *etc.* But when women fall away from the Lord, *invariably there is a man involved*. And many times, these men who are a stumbling block are strong in an ungodly and rebellious way. But at least, the women think, they are *strong*.

If a woman is unprotected by her father, she is in the desert, parched and thirsty. If she comes across an oasis with a sign saying that the water is bad, she will still be tempted to drink from it anyway. In our generation, *many* Christian men have abdicated their God-given role of assertive, humble strength. Christian women are left floundering as a result—especially when their fathers do not protect them. Consequently, Christian women will often pick a self-centered non-Christian man who is assertive, even if he is poison for her. She does this even though she has known many Christian men—nice guys who never assert anything. Many women are so hungry for initiative, leadership, and authority that they will put up with a lot of garbage for the sake of a counterfeit.

Fortunately, these are not the only two options. Women are not limited to Christian men who abdicate their masculinity, and ungodly men who abuse their masculinity through abusing women. There is a third option, even though it has become relatively rare within the last several generations. This is the man who is assertive and strong *for the sake of the other person.* He exercises his strength, not to get his own way, but to lead, help, and minister. He exercises authority the way Christ did—true authority with a servant's heart. This is the kind of young man a woman's parents should delight to see.

As the parents oversee the courtship of their daughter, they must be careful to maintain a hard-headed and realistic understanding of marriage. They must not seek a union for their daughter on sentimental grounds. This is not because sentiment is *wrong;* rather, sentiment is a poor foundation. This also is a matter of wisdom.

CHAPTER FIVE

Details of Courtship

If a young man shows interest in a girl and she has no interest in him (say, if he is the pizza delivery boy), she doesn't have to say "talk to my father," she can simply refuse him. But if he is an acquaintance and serious, she should send him to talk to her father.

Her father should hear the young man out. If the father knows that there is no way he would ever give permission, then he should graciously deny the young man's request to get to know his daughter better. If he thinks the young man has possibilities, then he should thank him, and tell him that he will get back to him within a few days. He should be *very gracious* with the young man. Talking to the father of the girl you like is a hard thing to do anyway, so the father should not make it unnecessarily difficult for the young man.

The father should obviously pray about the situation, and he should have a talk with both his wife and daughter. If he talks to his daughter, and she is simply not interested, under virtually all circumstances, the father should get back to the suitor and simply say *no*. If she has no interest in the young man, then the father should inform him that he does not have permission to court his daughter. The father should take great pains to be gracious, but firm. The protection this provides the daughter is obvious. When a girl says *no* to a young man, he often feels free to press her for her reasons. She may not have to date him, but she frequently has to debate him. When she gives a reason, he feels free to try to overcome that reason. "If that were different, *then* would you see me?" It is next to impossible for a young man to get away with doing this to the girl's father.

If the daughter is interested in the suitor, then the father should come back to him, and say, "No, you cannot take my daughter out, but you may take *us* out." Because there is interest, the young man is given permission to spend time with the family. If that goes well, he may begin to spend time alone with the daughter under the watchful oversight of the father. The young man is being invited to spend time with the family. Younger siblings get a good example of courtship lived out in front of them, but they have to be taught not to tease and laugh—at least not too much. One of the best ways to "sit on them" is to remind them that "their turn is coming."

These are not hard and fast rules. Depending on the circumstances, the father may give the young man permission to take his daughter to dinner, or to go out on what some people would call "a date." The point is not "how many times to the house before there is a proposal," but rather whether or not the father is being judicious and responsible. Sometimes a father would be foolish to give permission to date, and other times such permission is wise.

If the family is impressed and the young man continues to show interest in the daughter, he can begin spending more one-on-one time with her under the father's oversight. Once he becomes "part of the family," it is still not wise to send the daughter off into the dark in an automobile with the young man, and say, "Be back in six hours." People can get in all kinds of trouble in six hours. He should be permitted to spend time with her in accountable settings, whether at home or out on a date. In all ways, he is accountable to the family, and primarily to the father.

If it becomes obvious during the courtship that the young man is not suitable, then it is the father's duty to explain to him that he is not free to continue to come around in the same way. He no longer has the father's permission to single his daughter out in the way he has been doing. If this becomes necessary, the father should be extremely gracious (and equally firm). When it is clear to the father that a marriage is not going to result from this courtship, *nothing will be gained* by postponing the hard discussion with the suitor.

Obviously a young man is not going to go through all this unless he is thinking seriously about marriage. As the relationship progresses, he should then come to the father and ask for his daughter's hand in marriage. If he does not seem to be getting anywhere (and if he has had enough time for a reasonable man to make up his mind), the father should take him aside and ask him. If he is an agreeable suitor with cold feet, the father should give him a nudge. If he has come to have doubts about the whole thing, then the father should graciously give him his way out, and show him the door.

But under normal circumstances, everyone should be agreeable to a marriage, and a date will be set for the wedding.

The Wedding

When everything has gone well, a date for the wedding will be set. As established above, the wedding is an exchange of covenant vows surrounding a sexual relationship, which results in the establishment of a public marriage covenant. God has put this man and woman together, and man has no authority on his own to dissolve it according to his own autonomous opinions.

Once the decision to marry is made, parents should take care not be distracted by the liturgy of the wedding. The wedding is simply a doorway into the house of the marriage. There is no problem with "decorating" this doorway—the practice of adorned brides and plenty of wine for the guests is certainly biblical—so the parents of the bride should feel free to spend some money and have a joyful wedding. But many are so attached to "weddings" that they may find themselves frantically trashing the inside of the house for the sake of decorating the doorway. This sin affects the pleasantness of the home being established. Parents should not let these external things distract them from the important thing that God is establishing—a new household.

One of the best ways to keep a proper focus during a wedding is to keep the wedding covenantal, and to keep a biblical doctrinal perspective clear throughout the wedding. This is best done by understanding the various roles *in a biblical wedding* of the various governments involved.

God has established three governments among men—the first being the government of the family. This was established in Eden, and is the basic building block of the other two governments which God has ordained—the government of the church, and that of the civil magistrate.

In courtship and marriage, the central government is obviously that of the family. In a wedding, the family is giving birth; it is reproducing itself. The transaction is occurring between representatives of two families, coming together to establish a new, third family.

According to the Bible, the other two governments have authority at a wedding as well, but that authority may not be what many might assume. First, with regard to the church, Protestant Christians usually do not think of their ministers as performing any priestly functions, *except at weddings*. But marriage is not a sacrament; it is a covenant vow surrounding a lawful sexual relationship. The Bible teaches that vows before the Lord are not to be made lightly, the church therefore has an interest in *witnessing* these vows, and insisting that they be kept.

All governments are ministerial—not legislative. Neither the state nor the church is permitted by God to invent or make up laws. They are both charged by God, in their respective spheres, to administer and apply the laws that God has given in his Word. So the church does have a legitimate interest in the proceedings of a wedding and should therefore have a ministerial representative present and involved. Adultery, for example, is an offense which should be disciplined by the church. But the church cannot discipline for this unless it knows who is married to whom. So the elders of the church do have a legitimate role. They are witnessing vows which have ecclesiastical ramifications for all members of the church. Unless the church acknowledges and understands who is married to whom, the word *adultery* becomes meaningless. Because of the solemnity and gravity of the vows, it is entirely appropriate for a minister of the church to be present to *administer* the vows, and to serve as the witness on behalf of the church. However, this is not a sacerdotal or priestly function. When he "pronounces" them husband and wife, it should be done in such a way that it does not appear that he is *making* them husband and wife, but rather *declaring* the results of the vows which he, and all others present, have witnessed.

This is all a matter of observing and witnessing and ratifying the vows. The church is authoritatively observing the authoritative action of the families. The church says to the couple, "We have heard you, we have observed you, and we declare to this assembled congregation that you have exchanged your vows of marriage. This is not because we have created this marriage, but because we have witnessed your vows before God." This is done in a public way and everyone is held accountable. The wedding is the best place for this declaration to be made.

The civil magistrate also has a legitimate and necessary role in weddings. A covenant is being made—a binding covenant—and it is a covenant that involves *property, inheritance,* and the *custody of children.* When a quarrel erupts between citizens over such things, biblically the civil magistrate has the arbitrating position. The situation is not altered if the disputants happen to be married. Suppose a man deserts his wife, and in doing so, he steals her endowment. Clearly, the magistrate must be involved in the resolution of the dispute. But if the magistrate has no knowledge of the covenant that was made, then he is required to arbitrate a dispute which he cannot arbitrate. This means that the magistrate must have a representative at the wedding also, who then records the results of the wedding in a way that the magistrate can recognize. Traditionally, the minister of the church has been deputized to perform this civil function, but another representative would do as well. It would perhaps be better to have a distinction of representatives so that the congregation may maintain these important distinctions in their minds.

The civil magistrate also has a role when people attempt to marry within bounds prohibited by Scripture. In such situations, the magistrate has the responsibility to intervene— *e.g.*, in a godly society, the current attempts to solemnize sodomite unions would be broken up by the police. The legitimate role of the civil magistrate is one of witnessing familial vows which necessarily have civil ramifications.

So the civil magistrate does have a legitimate, scriptural role at the formation of a marriage, although not the role that it currently *thinks* it has. If a property dispute broke out between two neighbors, the civil magistrate is competent to deal with that. However, the civil magistrate is not the owner of all property, and therefore the dispenser of it, but rather the umpire of disputes between owners of property. In our statist society, we often think the civil government has more authority than the Bible teaches. But the state *should* be the umpire in certain areas. Because marriage involves issues like property, inheritance, and heirs, the civil magistrate must be formally notified of the marriage before he can be an impartial referee if and when necessary. This means he must have some representative or deputy present when a marriage covenant is made.

Although the civil magistrate does have a legitimate role to play, the tyrannical role our modern state has assumed can be seen in such terminology as marriage "licenses." The modern idolatrous state assumes authority over everything; Christians too often acquiesce in that usurpation. Our civil government is becoming increasingly tyrannical, and it thinks it has the authority to license us to do *anything*. When couples go to get a marriage license, they must recognize that the state does not *own* the right to get married. If the civil government collapsed, marriages could still lawfully be formed and consummated under God. If two Christians desire to marry, and God's law permits such a marriage, the state has no authority to forbid it. The authority to forbid comes from the Bible, and not from the legislative authority of the licensing magistrate.

It must always be remembered that at a biblical wedding, the principal authority is being exercised by the family of the bride, and to a lesser extent, the groom and family of the groom. A young Christian man, and a young Christian virgin, with the blessing of their respective families, make a vow in the presence of representatives of the church and the civil order. They are held publicly accountable by these other governments for the vows they have taken. But this accountability is not originative; in both cases it is ministerial.

Miscellaneous Concerns and Questions

Biblical principles of courtship and marriage must be *obeyed* in order to do any good. Mere assent is not good enough. "But be doers of the word, and not hearers only, deceiving yourselves" (James 1:22). If biblical knowledge is not put into practice, a mere listening to true information is *deceptive*. Nowhere is this truth more evident than in the biblical teaching on courtship and marriage. There appears to be an inverse relationship between the number of books and seminars on successful relationships on the one hand, and the number of successful marriages on the other.

Being married *amplifies* what a person is. If someone is mature in his Christianity, he or she will be mature whether single or married. Many are miserable and single. Their problems range from sexual temptation to loneliness, and they think that marriage will fix all their problems. But when they marry, they find it is like getting plugged into an amplifier with the volume turned all the way up. There is nothing like marriage to reveal how *selfish* a person really is. And such selfishness can easily be hidden under the emotions that come with being in love. Often guys will say, "I love Susie." This does not necessarily mean they are interested in Susie's best interest, but rather, "I really like the sensations which occur *in me* whenever Susie is around." When a boy says, "I love ice cream" he is not seeking the ice cream's best interest. He loves the sensation ice cream gives him. In short, he loves *himself.*

When someone is single, he can assume he is far more spiritually mature than he really is. It is easy for his or her parents to fall mistakenly into the same assumption. It is consequently very important for the single person to be a growing, maturing Christian before marriage.

Like all relationships with fellow creatures, the husband/wife relationship is a *horizontal one.* The Bible teaches us that our primary duty is with our *vertical* relationship with God. We are to love Him first, above all others. His Word is to be obeyed, and put into practice as we love others. But obedience to His Word includes obedience to the principles of courtship and biblical marriage.

One of the central problems with modern teaching about courtship and marriage (including much Christian teaching) is that the emphasis is horizontal. But the key to God-honoring marriages is for the husband and wife to honor God *above all.* God is to be first. Those who genuinely love God the Father through His Son Jesus Christ know what their duties to their spouse are.

Problems in marriage are *always* the result of self-centeredness. In other words, husbands and wives do not get along because of *sin.* Couples who are in fellowship with God know how to maintain fellowship with one another. Couples who do not know how to walk with God cannot say the same. Oftentimes when couples get married, they will make decisions in a couple-centered fashion, rather than in a God-centered fashion. In doing this, they are planting the seeds of many future problems. There is nothing wrong with our desires, provided they are surrendered to God.

So the time a person spends when he is single should be time spent in preparation for marriage. This is important even if he never gets married. This is because biblical preparation for marriage is nothing more than learning to follow Jesus

Christ and to love one's neighbor. In other words, preparation for Christian marriage is basically the same as preparation for Christian living. Christians are to prepare for marriage by learning self-denial, subduing their pride, and putting their neighbor first. Once they learn to love God and love their neighbor, they are prepared to enter into the covenant of marriage with one of their neighbors. These are issues which should be in the forefront of every parent's mind as their children approach the age when they may court and marry.

Possible Objections to Courtship

We have shown that parents have a true authority over "matters of the heart." In using the phrase "matters of the heart," we must remember that in our culture we tend to think the "heart" is that which has all true authority. In matters of the heart, how can anyone *else* come in and tell someone what to do? We think that romance is the authority, or that happy endings are. But biblically speaking, this is entirely erroneous.

The objection will certainly be made that parents can make mistakes. This is certainly the case—this is a fallen world, and parents can and do make mistakes. But so can the heart, so can the emotional response of the woman, so can the emotional impetus that causes a man to pursue a woman, so can young couples in the grip of sexual temptation. All these have fallen, and erred, and sinned. In considering what we are to do, the issue is not, "Can we make mistakes in this way?" but rather, "What does the *Bible* teach?" As we have seen, the biblical examples of parental authority include parents who have not done everything they ought to have done.

Another objection that will occur to many is this: "How can we require our children to do what *we* did not do?" Parents may be wondering if their behavior during courtship (or lack of courtship) disqualifies them from teaching their children in this area. The biblical answer to this is, "By no means"—we are to teach our children the law of Christ, and not our own personal experiences. Our experience may be used to help us teach God's law, but our experience does not "set the curriculum." The Bible does.

Even though most parents who are preparing children for courtship did not get together by means of courtship, they are not therefore disqualified. This is how it has to be as we return to any older cultural practice like courtship. This custom is being restored among Christians. Courtship used to be very much a part of our culture, but it is now a cultural practice that has fallen into almost total disuse, and, as a consequence, virtually no one knows anything about it. Therefore, virtually every married reader of this book did not get married as a result of the pattern of courtship. Not surprisingly, this question has occurred to some readers, and perhaps the same question has occurred to their sons or daughters. A son or daughter may say, "I've heard the story of how you two got together—so what are you putting this on *me* for?"

The basic answer is that the Bible teaches what we are to do, and our experience cannot set the curriculum of what we are to teach our children. We teach to our children what the Bible teaches. If parents had a really good biblical experience in their courtship, then that experience provides good practical wisdom in teaching what the Bible says. But if the parents have not had that experience, they are *not* therefore disqualified from teaching their children what the Bible says. To take an extreme example, many parents were not sexually pure before they got married. Does this disobedience of theirs mean they must permit similar disobedience from their children? The Bible sets the standards of sexual morality and sexual purity. Parents are not to teach what they *did* as normative— unless, biblically, it was. Parents who have kept themselves pure are in a far better position to teach what the Bible requires, but all parents are required to teach *the same standard*. If the obedience of the parents corresponds with the teaching of Bible, then that is a very great blessing. But this blessing is not part of the parents' qualifications for teaching. Parents teach their children because God requires it. In other words, such things are not requirements of the parents which *they* came up with; they are from the Word of God. Parents do not have to defend it or apologize for it; if they see it in the Word, then they should pass it on to their children.

Another question might be, "How does our family get to know these other young people?" At the risk of sounding simplistic, parents should get to know young people *through having them into their homes*. Parents of young people should be hospitable to other young people. In doing this, however, they should be careful to guard against some sort of unsupervised quasi-dating. The groups included in the home for social activities should not be "setups" where two girls and two guys are not *exactly* together, but they all know who goes with whom. Six kids, with three girls and three boys, is technically "a group" but it can quickly turn into something else. Parents should strive for a warm home environment, which is relatively risk-free. In such a setting, the kids can get to know one another without developing any *ad hoc* commitments. In doing this, odd numbers, and different age groups (within reason) will help quite a bit.

Of course, the practice of courtship does not turn the world into a perfect place. Some young people will have trouble in group situations, but this is not really a problem with guy/girl relations. Suppose a pretty girl does nothing more than to say, "Hi," to some poor kid, and he immediately says to himself, "She *cares*; she *likes* me." He is then crushed when she greets someone else in the same way. This is certainly a problem, but it is not a relationship problem—rather it is a personal problem. If someone insists on building up imaginary relationships in his mind, a group setting will not help much. This, however, is a character flaw, and not a problem with the group, or with the other young people. If someone gets hurt as a result of their own daydreaming, then that young person needs teaching, encouragement, and admonition from his parents on a personal level.

When Christian parents are hospitable to their children's

friends, this will prevent the assumption that "if my children don't date recreationally, the only alternative we are left with is picking the name of their future spouses out of the phone book, or maybe, if we are lucky, out of the church directory." There are *many* ways of getting to know others apart from recreational dating. In many group situations a young person gets to know the other person far better than he would in a dating situation. Dating is not the best way to get to know another person, but it is the best way to get involved with the other person. When a guy asks a girl out and she agrees, she doesn't try to think of ways to make the worst first impression possible. He thinks the same way; he wants to make a good impression too. But apart from a scriptural wisdom and maturity, it is much more difficult for someone to know what is going to impress another person in a group situation. If a guy takes a girl to dinner, he can say complimentary things— that always goes over well. Virtually everyone knows the rules for making good impressions in a dating situation. But in a group, an individual's little acts of selfishness *directed toward someone else entirely*, and not the person in whom he is interested, will reveal volumes about him.

If a girl wants to be impressed with a young man, she needs to see how he speaks to his own mother at home, and not how nice he can be across the dinner table from a cute girl at a restaurant. If she wants to know how he will speak to her as a wife in ten or fifteen years (and if she is taught well by her father, she *should* want to know), she should look very closely at how he talks to his mother. She will not learn this at the prom, when he is "putting his best foot forward" and she is doing the same. They may both deceive themselves into thinking that if they date in this way they are getting to know the other person. In a sense this is true; they *are* getting to know the other person, but they are getting attached to them *first*. Before they get to know one another, while they are still putting up appearances, they are growing attached. This means that when they learn how the other person really is (and they certainly will eventually), they are then in the difficult position of not being able to leave without hurt.

So parents can prevent this through having the "gang" over. And when other parents do the same, parents should let their kids go to their homes. Social group gatherings are simultaneously informative and practical.

When a couple pairs off, and the guy encourages an emotional response from the girl, and he gets that response, then their attachment was a result of what they both were doing. By the time they find out what they wanted to know before *formally* attaching, they discover they are already *informally* attached. For example, many years ago, a young man came to me for some advice. He could not have done a finer job of getting his girlfriend prepared to agree to marry him. It appeared that he had been deliberately working on it, but when he asked me his questions it revealed that he had not been doing anything of the kind. Having done all the ground work, he then came to me and said, "How do you know if someone is the right one?" Like a dog chasing a fire truck, many guys don't know what to do when they catch it. This young man didn't have a clue. He didn't have any objective grounds for doing what he was doing. His girlfriend was assuming that he knew what he was doing, which was a bad mistake. She was assuming that he was initiating on purpose and intelligently, and so she was emotionally responsive. The problem here was the system of pairing off through recreational dating.

This is not a good system. The covenantal fence protects young people. The marriage covenant *protects*. No one can go into a marriage relationship to find out what it would be like to be married to this person *without being married to them already*. This means that with the scriptural system of courtship, the commitment comes first, and true intimate knowledge of the spouse comes second. We are not to find out what the other is like in every detail first and *then* make the commitment. The logic of unbelieving dating resembles a "test run" more than the courtship of a Christian virgin. Because of this test run mentality, it is not surprising that immorality is so prevalent. If a man needs to know a woman *before* he makes a commitment, then why should he be denied the privilege of getting to know what she is like in bed? In God's pattern, wisdom is exercised as public information about a suitor, or about a young woman, is carefully gathered. All intimacy follows the commitment; in the biblical pattern *no* intimacy precedes the commitment.

Another possible problem is that of jealousy. In the area of courtship (*and* group social gatherings), parents should beware of various jealousies or competitions *among the parents*. In Colossians 3:12–13, we find a general principle applying to a Christian's relationships with all other believers. The *general* principle also applies *specifically* to how we behave as our sons grow up, leave our homes, and take their wives. This principle is that we are to be "putting on tender mercies, being humble in mind, meek, long-suffering, bearing with one another." This is important and necessary in all our relations, but especially here. When a man initiates and a woman responds with her father's approval, everything is wonderful. But often, if the young lady is attractive, more than one man is interested, and there is the obvious possibility of competition and rivalry.

Now the fact that parents are involved in the courtship process doesn't remove the temptation for such jealousies. For example, with the recreational dating system, if a man is interested in a particular girl and he asks her out, and someone else wants to do the same thing, he may be jealous. But as a Christian, he knows that she is not committed in any covenantal way to him, or to the other guy. Consequently, his jealousy has no grounds and he knows it. The Bible teaches that within the marriage covenant husbands *ought* to be jealous; godly jealousy is required for the protection of the covenantal marriage fence (2 Cor. 11:2). Obviously, if there is no covenant, then there are no biblical grounds for jealousy— there is no covenantal commitment, and therefore there can be no covenantal betrayal. Therefore it is easy for a young Christian man to see his jealousy is unwarranted in dating situations. Of course, the situation changes when a couple has seen each other regularly. Then full jealousy can easily rage *without* covenantal warrant because they are both operating on the basis of an informal, unspoken covenant. Such covenants are no protection at all, but they do help make things messier.

Because the problem is *overt*, a young Christian man in the situation described above knows that his competitive jealousy is not right; it is ungodly. But in a courtship situation, *parents* may find themselves subjected to similar temptations, and may be less on guard against it because all their concerns are "altruistic"—they want what is best for someone else, their son or daughter. Because it is on behalf of *another*, it does not seem to them to be self-centered. The parents feel the way they do out of a concern for someone else; it is nothing more than parental love. Because the strife is on behalf of another (their son or daughter), it may not be as easy to identify the emotions as sin—but it is pernicious sin nonetheless. Every potential spouse everywhere else in the world has the perfect right to be perfectly and completely uninterested in one's daughter or son *without giving offense*. If such a lack of interest offends, then the parents are being possessive of someone outside of the boundaries of a covenant relationship. And *that* is sin.

The Garden

As my horse trotted wearily up the road, I could see the walls of a beautiful garden ahead. Outside the gate was an equally beautiful woman. At the sound of my greeting, she turned and dropped a curtsey. "Good sir . . . good morning."

I looked at her, and then at the garden walls extending out to the right and left. Behind her was the garden gate.

I said, "I am very thirsty . . . for something clean."

She smiled, and her smile made me thirstier still. But she said nothing.

"Is there water here?" I asked.

"There is a stream within my garden." Her statement was simply a statement of fact; there was no invitation at all in it.

I asked, "May I come in and drink?"

"No," she said. "The lord of my mother's garden doe.; not permit that."

"Why is this? Other women have let me drink from the gardens that they tend." I glanced at the fruit-laden branches which were visible over the top of the garden wall. "You have a lovely garden, but those who let me drink had gardens just as beautiful."

She laughed at this, and her laugh was merry indeed.

"I have no doubt that you have been in some lovely gardens. But was the water clean?"

"No," I said, and in spite of myself, turned my head and looked down. She continued with a question. "Is that why you are no longer in the gardens tended by these women?"

I was ashamed so I did not answer her. Instead I looked past her into the garden. The path through the gate disappeared after a few feet, leaving the view of anyone on the road.

"It seems like a shame for such a garden to go to waste."

She seemed both puzzled and amused. "How does it go to waste?"

"Does any man drink from your stream?"

"No, but no man fouls it either."

"But is that not a waste? Was not your stream made to quench the thirst of travelers?"

"I'm afraid you are seriously mistaken. It was made to quench the thirst, not of travelers, but of the lord of the garden."

"Oh," I said, "This garden has a lord?"

"No," she said.

"Then I don't understand. Are you speaking in riddles?"

She smiled. "No, I do not. The garden will one day have a lord, although it does not yet. The stream is for him alone."

"And who will your lord be?"

"When my mother's lord gives a blessing, the one whom I appoint."

"How can the lesser appoint the greater?"

"How can it not be so? When my lord comes, I will grant to him my garden. But until I do, he is just another traveler."

"And what do you look for? I am sure there are many who knock at your gate."

At this she blushed slightly but looked straight at me. "I will not have a lord who does not have a lord himself—my lord must have taken an oath of fealty to the Landlord."

"The Landlord? Who is he?"

"He is the owner of all the gardens along this road. In order to come into my garden, my lord must take an oath before the Landlord to tend the garden well. He must also swear that he will enter no other garden."

I had never heard such words as these before. "How long must he stay out of other gardens?"

"Forever."

"But what if he is born to travel?"

"Then he is not born for my garden."

"I see," I said, becoming a little angry. "Then why have I never heard of such an oath? I have been in many gardens."

"Yes, you said that before. But was the water clean? Were the gardens tended? That is what happens when there is no oath."

"So that is all? If someone takes an oath before this Landlord, you will make them your lord?"

"No."

"Well, what else then?"

"There are many men who think they can tend my garden well, and who would be willing to swear an oath before the Landlord saying so. But that does not mean that my mother's lord, or I, share their confidence."

"What do you mean?"

"I mean that I know the extent of the garden. I have a knowledge of it that cannot be gained from the road. But no man can share that knowledge until after I have made him my lord and husband. So I must have the measure of the man before."

"So what must a man do? It seems like much work."

She smiled once again. "There is much work. There is also much fruit."

"So what must a man do?"

"The first thing is to—"

"Yes, I know. He must swear to the Landlord. But after?"

"He must return to me, and ask to see my mother's lord."

"And what would he say?"

"That depends on the man." At this parting comment, she turned and walked slowly back into the garden, pulling the gate closed behind her. I spurred my horse, which began to trot down the road. I did not know what to think, but I needed to find this Landlord.